Donna Fletcher

the FRANTIC MOTHER COOKBOOK

Illustrated by Nate Owens

HARVEST HOUSE PUBLISHERS
Eugene, Oregon 97402

THE FRANTIC MOTHER COOKBOOK

Copyright © 1982 Donna Fletcher Crow
Eugene, Oregon 97402
Library of Congress Catalog Card Number 82-081918
ISBN 0-89081-356-6

Printed in the United States of America.

FOR MY MOTHER
Who never lost her poise and dignity,
or her faith—even when I was a teenager.

About the Author

Donna Fletcher Crow lives in Boise, Idaho, with her attorney-writer husband and 4 children; Stanley, in high school; Preston in junior high; John, in grade school; and Elizabeth in diapers.

About *THE FRANTIC MOTHER COOKBOOK* she says, "People ask me how I thought of those things. Think of them? I lived them. It's straight autobiography. Not even the names are changed —there are no innocents."

Other Books by Donna Fletcher Crow
Recipes for the Protein Diet

TABLE OF CONTENTS

1

BAKE IT FAST

Friday Night

"Hey, Mom, I forgot to tell you, I invited my Sunday school class over for a party tonight."

"That's lovely, dear. But it's Johnny's birthday. I have ten six-year-olds in the family room right now. How about some other time?"

Doorbell rings.

"Too late, Mom. Hi, guys. Come on in. Refreshments will be a little late; my brother's having a party, too. We can play records while we wait."

"Will *somebody* pick up Elizabeth? She's crying."

Brownies for a Bunch

Turn oven to 350°. Put 4 squares *unsweetened chocolate* in ovenproof bowl and pop in oven. Spray 9" x 13" pan with Pam (or grease with shortening). In big mixer bowl dump 2 cubes margarine, *4 eggs,* 1 cup *sugar.* Beat smooth. Add 1 cup *flour* (don't bother to sift), 2 teaspoons *vanilla,* and melted chocolate. (Careful, just because they're ravenous and you're tired, don't burn your fingers.) Stir. Pour into a pan. Smooth with spatula. Lick spatula. Pop brownies into oven for half an hour. Wash dishes, fold laundry, and nurse baby while waiting. Put brownies in freezer to cool before icing—don't set on top of ice cream.

If you're really frantic, frost with canned icing. If you can manage it, making your own is cheaper and better. In mixing bowl, place: 1 box *powdered sugar,* 1 cube *margarine,* 6 tablespoons *cocoa,* 1 teaspoon *vanilla,* and ¼ cup *milk.* Beat slowly, then fast. You may need to add more milk, but go easy—even frantic moms don't want runny icing.

Cookies for Kids

Put in biggest mixing bowl: 2 cubes *margarine,* 1 cup *brown sugar* (mashed down), 1 cup *white sugar,* 2 *eggs.* Beat up well. Stir in with wooden spoon: 2 cups *flour* (unsifted), 1 teaspoon *soda,* 1 teaspoon *baking powder,* dash *salt,* 1 teaspoon *vanilla,* 2 tablespoons *water,* 2 cups *oatmeal,* (part wheat germ if you're into sneaky nutrition), 2 cups *cereal*—any kind (here's your chance to use up something the kids won't eat), and 1 cup *chocolate chips, coconut, or nuts* (they'll last longer if you use coconut or nuts; kids don't like them as well).

Drop globs on cookie sheet and bake 10 minutes at 350°. Or relieve the frenzy by spreading in two greased 9'' x 13'' pans (don't worry about getting dough clear to edges) and bake 20 minutes. Cut in squares.

When's Dessert Ready? Cake

In large saucepan dump: 1 cube *margarine*, ½ cup *oil*, 2 squares *unsweetened chocolate*, 1 cup *water*. Set over low heat to melt while you put 2 cups unsifted *flour*, 1 teaspoon *soda*, 2 cups *sugar*, 2 *eggs*, 1 teaspoon *cinnamon*, and 1 teaspoon *vanilla* in a big bowl. Put 1½ teaspoons *vinegar* in ½ cup measure and fill with *milk*. Put in bowl with flour; add melted mixture. Beat and pour in greased broiler pan. Bake 25 minutes at 350°.

In same saucepan (no need to wash it) put 1 stick *margarine*, 2 squares *unsweetened chocolate* and 6 tablespoons *milk*. Put on *low* heat and let melt while cake bakes. Sit down and read Virtue magazine. Remove cake from oven and pan from heat. Put 1 box *powdered sugar*, 1 teaspoon *vanilla* and ½ cup package *pecan bits* into pan with melted chocolate and beat. Pour over cake and eat.

2
LICKETY-SPLIT SUNDAY DINNER

Sunday Morning

"Honey, where are my cuff links?"

"Sorry, in my drawer. I borrowed them a couple of days ago. Who was on the phone?"

"The pastor. Emergency board meeting at three o'clock this afternoon. So we'll have to eat *right* after church. He mentioned that his wife is out of town, so I invited him to dinner. Knew you'd want me to . . . Did you know you have a run in your stocking?"

"Hey, Mom. Colin's going to church with me. He can come for dinner, too, can't he? . . . Did you know you have a run in your stocking?"

"Will somebody pick up Elizabeth! She's crying again."

Oven Chicken
Empty 1 can *cream of chicken soup*, 1 can *cream of celery soup*, and 1 can *cream of mushroom soup*

into large saucepan. Stir in 1 can *water* and 1 cube *butter*. Heat until butter melts. Take out 1 cup of the sauce; stir 1½ cups *rice* (I use brown) into remainder. Pour into 9" x 13" casserole. Put 8 *chicken breasts* on top. Pour reserved sauce over. Bake uncovered at 275° for 3 hours.

Curried Fruit

Drain on paper towels: 1 can *pineapple slices*, 1 can *pear halves.* Arrange in baking pan and add *maraschino cherries* for color. Melt together: ⅔ cup *brown sugar*, ⅓ cup *butter*, and 2 teaspoons *curry powder.* Pour over fruit and bake uncovered at 350° for 45 minutes.

Oven-Baked Peas

Empty 2 packages (10-oz.) *frozen peas* into small casserole. Top with 2 tablespoons *margarine.* Cover tightly. Bake at 350° for 45 minutes with curried fruit.

Dump Cake

Pop this in the oven before you sit down to dinner, and it will be ready when you are—all nice and warm from the oven.

In 9" x 13" pan spread in layers: 1 can *cherry pie filling*, 1 can *crushed pineapple* (undrained), 1 box *yellow cake mix*, 1 cup *coconut.* Cut 1 stick *margarine* into bits and sprinkle over top. Bake at 350° for 1 hour. Serve with *ice cream.*

3

LADIES LUNCHEON

The Night Before

"Telephone, Mom. It's Mrs. Jones. She has the flu, and wants to know—Can the missionary ladies come to your house for lunch? She says just salad and rolls or something will be enough. Seems to me like you ought to give them some dessert, too . . . Mom, say something, she's waiting."

"Will somebody pick up Elizabeth? She's still crying."

24-Hour Fruit Salad

Dump together in a large colander: 1 can *white cherries*, 2 cans *pineapple chunks*, 1 can *tangerines*. Drain well. Stir in 1 cup *sour cream*, 2 cups *miniature marshmallows*, and ½ cup *blanched almonds*. Regrigerate overnight.

This serves 6-8 people—you'll probably need to double it for the missionary ladies. Serve nice scoops on *lettuce leaves*.

Streusel Coffee Cake

Cream together in a large bowl: 1 cup *margarine*, 2 cups *sugar*, 2 *eggs*. Stir in 2 cups *flour* (I use presifted for everything), 1 teaspoon *baking powder*, a shake of *salt*, ½ teaspoon *vanilla*, ½ teaspoon *almond extract*, and 1 cup *sour cream*.

Spoon half of this into a greased and floured angle food cake pan. Combine 1 teaspoon *cinnamon*, 2 tablespoons *brown sugar*, and ¾ cup *chopped walnuts.* * Sprinkle over batter in pan. Spoon on rest of batter. Run knife blade zig-zag through batter to swirl streusel.

Bake at 350° for 1 hour. Cool in pan 10 minutes before inverting to remove.

*Walnuts are optional—every recipe for this luncheon calls for nuts—that's too much of a good thing.

Ice Cream Bombe

Spread ½ gallon *vanilla ice cream* in a large, flat pan—like a broiler pan. Top with ½ gallon *chocolate ice cream*. (Have ice cream softened a bit first and cut in slices to place in pan.) Place in freezer while you whip 2 cups *heavy cream* with ¼ cup *sugar* and 2 teaspoons *vanilla*. Chop 1 box *chocolate-covered mint patties* (green centers are prettiest) and ½ cup *walnut pieces*. Fold into whipped cream and spread over ice cream.

Freeze and cut into squares to serve. When I was a teenager my mother always kept a pan of this in the freezer for those ever-occurring emergencies.

Plan B

Instead of fruit salad, serve *fresh fruit*, a *cheese*

board, and a selection of interesting *crackers*. With lots of crackers you can get by without the coffee cake—but they'd love the cake.

Buy a selection of the freshest, ripest produce your market has to offer. Polish it and arrange it flowing from a tier tray in the center of your table. Include a small, sharp knife at each guest's place setting, and pass a tray of cheeses. Choose at least three varieties of cheese: Firm and tangy such as cheddar, caerphilly, or Swiss; medium-textured and mild such as colby, jack, and havarti; and smooth and creamy such as bonbel, port salut, or brie. Small cards inserted into cheese with toothpicks stating what kind it is will be appreciated.

This is lovely for a buffet, too—any time of day.

4

BUSY DAY DISHES

Busy Day Prayers

"This is the Day the Lord Has Made."
Dear God,
I've trusted You with my life. Help me trust You
with my day.

Correction

Dear God, I am so tired
And there's so much to do.
Thank you that
"As your strength is,
So shall your day be."

"No, my child.
As your day is,
So shall your strength be."

Stuffed Tomatoes

Mix 2 cups *cottage cheese* with 2 tablespoons
finely diced *onion*, ⅓ cup sliced *stuffed olives*, 2

teaspoons *parsely flakes* (or 4 teaspoons freshly snipped parsley), ¼ teaspoon *salt,* dash *pepper.*

Cut 4 *tomatoes* into wedges, leaving attached at bottom. Place ½ cup cottage cheese filling in each tomato. Top with a dollop of *mayonnaise.* Serve on *lettuce leaves.*

Perfect for a quickie luncheon with Sugar Cube Biscuits from Chapter 13.

Stew Meat Casserole

Put this on before you go shopping.

Put 1 pound *stew meat* (or round steak strips, or short ribs) in a 2-quart casserole. Cover with 1 can *golden mushroom soup* and 1 can *creamy onion soup,* undiluted. Cover and bake 5 hours at 275°. Add 1 can *mushroom pieces* with juice before serving, if desired.

Serve over *noodles, rice,* or *mashed potatoes.*

Swiss Dish

Fry 1 pound *hamburger* with 1 medium *onion,* chopped and 1 teaspoon *garlic powder.* Drain well. Put in 1½-quart casserole. Cover with a can of *ravioli,* ½ cup grated *cheddar cheese,* 1 can *mushroom soup,* and ½ cup more grated *cheese.* (Use part Swiss cheese, if you like.) Bake 1 hour at 350°.

Chili Beef Casserole

Brown 1 pound *hamburger* with 1 medium chopped *onion,* 1 teaspoon garlic *powder,* and 2 tablespoons *chili powder.* Stir in 1 can *chili-beef soup* and 1 cup *sour cream.*

Let meat mixture simmer a few minutes while you cook 2 cups *noodles* according to package directions. Drain. Grate 2 cups *jack cheese.*

Fill a 2-quart casserole with layers: Noodles, cheese, meat, noodles, cheese, meat, cheese. Bake at 350° for 45 minutes.

Corn Bread

Mix together just until blended: ¾ cup *sugar,* 2 *eggs,* 2 cups *flour,* 2¼ teaspoons *baking powder,* ¾ teaspoon *salt,* 1 cup *corn meal,* 1 tablespoon melted *butter,* and 1½ cups *milk.* Bake in a 9" x 9" pan for half an hour at 400°.

Serve half with Honey Butter (Chapter 5) and half with Little Weiner Shortcake Sauce (below).

Little Weiner Shortcake Sauce

Combine: 1 can *cream of chicken soup,* ½ cup *milk,* 1 package *frozen peas,* partially thawed, ¼ cup sliced *green onions,* 1 can *cream style corn,* ½ cup grated *cheddar cheese,* and 1 package *hot dogs,* cut in 1" pieces. Simmer until all is heated through, about 15 minutes. Serve on squares of buttered corn bread.

Frantic Mother Macaroni

Pour a lot of *macaroni* (2 or 3 cups) into a pot of rapidly boiling salted water. Boil gently for 10 minutes until tender. Drain. Over low heat stir in 1 cube *margarine* until melted. Stir in about 2 cups of whatever *cheese* you have in the refrigerator (American, jack, colby, cream, etc.). Reduce heat to warm. Cover pot, and stir occasionally to melt cheese in. If it seems sticky, add about ½ cup *milk.* Serve right from the pot with a wooden spoon.

You can reheat this on stove or in oven—you'll need to pour a little milk over it for warming up.

Vegetable Casserole

Sauté ½ cup chopped *onion*, ½ cup chopped celery, and ½ cup chopped *green pepper* in 4 tablespoons *margarine*. Add 1 can *French-cut green beans*, drained, and 1 can *white corn*, drained. Stir in 1 can *cream of celery soup* and ½ cup *sour cream*. Place in casserole. Crush ½ box *cheese crackers*, mix with 1 cube melted *margarine*, and sprinkle over top. Bake at 350° for half an hour.

Cole Slaw

Finely shred ½ head *cabbage*. Mince 2 teaspoons *onion*, and chop ½ *green pepper* and 2 stalks *celery*. In a small bowl stir together ½ cup *mayonnaise*, 1 tablespoon *sugar*, 2 teaspoons prepared *mustard*, and ¼ teaspoon *salt*. Lightly mix dressing into salad vegetables. Top with a sprinkling of *pepper*.

Praline Sundae Sauce

Combine 1¼ cups *brown sugar*, 1 cup *light cream*, 1⅓ cups *marshmallows*, and a dash of *salt* in heavy saucepan. Heat, stirring constantly until sugar dissolves and mixture comes to a boil. Cook over medium heat about 9 minutes (220° on candy thermometer). Remove from heat and add ¼ cup *butter*, 1 teaspoon *vanilla*, and ⅓ cup *walnut* or *pecan* pieces. Serve warm over ice cream.

5

DO-YOUR-OWN-THING MEALS

Do I Have to Eat That?

"Gotcha this time. You can't complain about the cooking if you make it yourself!"

"Oh, yes we can—*you* put the stuff out."

Buffet Pizzas

For every 4 pizzas you will need: 1 package large *flour tortillas*, soft *margarine*, 1 can *pizza sauce*, 8 ounces grated *Mozarella cheese*, a choice of toppings: Browned *hamburger*, drained *pineapple chunks*, sliced *pepperoni*, drained canned *shrimp*, *mushrooms*, sliced *olives*, chopped *green pepper*, etc.—you get the idea.

Spread 1 tortilla with margarine, place another tortilla on top—Presto—pizza crust! Spread with sauce, sprinkle with cheese and toppings.

Place in oven, right on the rack for about 10 minutes at 375°. Watch them closely and remove when they look done. Careful not to burn fingers when removing!

Salad Bar

Since only 2 or 3 pizzas can be baked at once, set out a big bowl of washed, dried*, bite-sized *salad greens*. Also set out smaller bowls of anything you have in your refrigerator for toppings: Raw or cooked *vegetables*, a can of *mixed vegetables*, a jar of *3-bean salad*, *sprouts*, chopped hard-boiled *eggs*, *cottage cheese*, *cheddar* chunks, *croutons*, etc. Sliced *pickled beets* are my favorite. Canned *asparagus spears* are great with hard-boiled eggs. Or try something exotic for a change: *Palm hearts*, *sliced water chestnuts*, *bamboo shoots*, marinated *artichoke hearts*, *mushrooms*, or *brussels sprouts*—but not all at once. And a choice of dressings, of course.

*No matter how much fun your topping choices are, the success of a salad rests on its greens. And it's crucial to have them *dry*. Since I have yet to meet the possessor of a French greens basket for spinning them dry, I'm eternally grateful to Adelle Davis, who suggested throwing your salad greens in a pillow case, closing with a tie-wire, and running them through the spin-dry cycle of your washing machine. And in all the years I've been doing it I only once goofed and ran them clear through the wash. Believe me, you don't want your greens *that* clean!

Top-Your-Own Waffles

Many years ago my family gave me a big waffle iron for Christmas and ever since, waffles have been one of our favorite Saturday night suppers. No waffle recipes follow because I've never found anything better than the *whole wheat and honey mix* on my grocer's shelf. Actually, any pancake recipe will work simply by separating the eggs and folding in stiffly-beaten whites at the lastminute.

For toppers we like: *Applesauce* with a sprinkle of *cinnamon-sugar;* fresh or frozen *berries* or *peach* slices with *sour cream* or *whipped cream;* a variety of *syrups*—the kids like maple, my husband likes fruit flavored, and my favorite is **Honey Butter:** Beat until fluffy: 1 cube *margarine* (of course butter would be lovely, I just never have it on hand), and ½ cup *creamy clover honey.* Regular honey would work, but if you can find this creamy white kind in your grocery store it's really special.

This recipe alone is worth the price of the book; it's better than catsup—kids will eat *anything* with Honey Butter on it!

Tacos

Grate a BIG bowl of *cheese* (cheddar or jack)—bet you can't grate enough that they won't ask for refills.

Fry a LOT of *hamburger* on which you've shaken *salt, pepper, garlic, oregano,* and *chili powder.* That's the trouble with tacos—with that much hamburger you could make a casserole that'd last 3 nights—but they'd rather have the tacos.

Heat a can of *refried beans* gently, adding a bit of *water.* They stick very easily. Set out bowls of sliced *olives, onions* (if anyone likes them), shredded *lettuce,* chopped tomatoes, catsup, hot sauce, and *sour cream.*

Have hard and soft shells both. *Hard shells* you

just buy and set out. For soft shells buy *corn tortillas* and heat ½-inch of *cooking oil* in a small skillet until very hot. With tongs place 1 torilla in oil, count to four (tortilla will puff), turn with tongs and count to four. Place on paper towel. **Repeat and repeat and repeat, stacking between** paper towels. The tricky part is guessing how many they'll eat. I've never found a satisfactory way to warm up leftover tortillas.

6

FAMILY NIGHT FOOD FAVORITES

Family Night

"But why can't I go to Curtis's?"

"Do we really have to go through this again?"

"But Mom—"

"The mere fact that God put us together in the same house with the same blood lines does not make us a family. A family is made by sharing experiences—doing things together. This is a recording."

"But we spend Sunday night together. Why do we have to spend Saturday night together, too? One night a week is enough."

"Apparently not. You just referred to your brother as 'what's-his-name.' "

Make-it-yourself dishes from Chapter 5 are great for family times. Here are some more we like:

French Toast Fondue

Cut 1 loaf *French bread* into bite-sized cubes, with crust on each one. Beat 2 *eggs*, ½ cup *milk*, and ¼ teaspoon *salt* together.

Heat *cooking oil* (a couple of inches deep) and ½ teaspoon *salt* in fondue pot. Each person dips a chunk of bread in milk and egg mixture, then fries it golden in fondue pot. (If you don't have a fondue pot, use electric skillet.)

Dip bites in *powdered sugar, syrup,* or *Honey Butter* (Chapter 5).

"No, John! Don't eat off the fondue fork, you'll burn your . . . too late. Sorry."

Treasure Hunt Fudge

This is the famous See's Fudge recipe—it can't be improved on. Put in saucepan: 12 *marshmallows*, 1 small can *evaporated milk*, (⅔ cup), and 2 cups *sugar*. Bring to a boil, stirring constantly and boil exactly 6 minutes. Continue to stir while it boils. Do not stir with rubber spatula—it will melt. Guess how I know.

Have a big bowl ready with 1 package *chocolate chips*, 1 teaspoon *vanilla*, and ¾ cube *butter* in it. 1 cup *nuts*, too, if you like. Pour the hot mixture over ingredients in bowl. Let stand a few minutes to melt. Beat well by hand. Pour into 8" x 8" pan and cool until firm. Cut in 1" squares.

For treasure hunt, wrap squares of fudge in foil. Give each person a portion of the candy and an assigned area of the house or yard. They are to hide the candy (all in a klump or each piece separately) and write clues to its whereabouts. Everyone exchanges clues and hunts. Then EAT. Warning: If you have a dog, tie him up.

Philosophy: Family Night food should be EASY—Mother is part of the family, too.

Sneaky Clam Chowder

In a big pot fry 6 strips of *bacon*, crisp. Remove and crumble. In bacon fat, fry 1 chopped *onion*. Dump in 3 cans *cream of potato soup*, 2 cans *minced clams*, with liquid, 1½ soup cans *milk*, season with *salt* and *pepper*, and heat.

My husband and I like it topped with *butter*, *parsley*, and *paprika*; the kids don't. We all like it topped with crumbled bacon, though. *Chowder crackers* are fun, too.

Sneakier Yet Chili

Heat together a giant can of *chili with beans* and a smaller can of *chili without beans*. Serve with do-it-yourself (again) toppings: *Hot sauce, catsup*, chopped *green onions*, chopped *olives*, grated *cheddar cheese, sour cream.*

Real Homemade Chili

For the real thing, brown 4 pounds coarsely *ground beef chuck*, 1 large *onion* chopped, and 2 cloves *garlic*, minced. Add 1 teaspoon *oregano*, 1 teaspoon *cumin*, 2 heaping tablespoons *chili powder*, 4 teaspoons *salt*, ¼ teaspoon *pepper*, 2 cans (1 pound each) *whole tomatoes*. Bring to a boil and simmer 45 minutes. Skim off fat. Add 1 large can *kidney beans*, drained, if desired.

Cheese-Easy Fondue

Heat 1 (16-oz.) jar *Cheese Whiz* and 1 cube *margarine* in fondue pot until smooth and melted. Dip chunks of crusty *French bread, cherry tomatoes*, cubes of *red apples*.

Use leftovers in cheese omelette.

Party Popcorn

Pop about 1½ cups *popcorn*. Remove unpopped kernels. You should have about 6 quarts popcorn. Melt 1 cup *light brown sugar* and 1 cup *margarine* together. Stir into popcorn with ¾ teaspoon *salt* until well coated. Bake 10 minutes at 350°, stirring once or twice. Cool before serving.

This is great with a cup or two of toasted *pecan halves* or whole *blanched almonds*, but awfully expensive and the kids won't appreciate it. Try stirring in a large bag of *M&M's* for variety.

Dessert Fondue

Combine 1 (14-oz.) can *sweetened condensed milk*, 1 (6-oz.) package *butterscotch chips*, 1 (6-oz.) package *chocolate chips*, 1 jar (7-oz.) *marshmallow cream*, ⅓ cup *milk*, 1 tablespoon *butter*, and 1 teaspoon *vanilla* in fondue pot. Heat and stir until smooth. Stir in ½ cup *coconut* flakes if desired.

Dip: *Fruit pieces*—banana, apple, pear, grapes, peaches, pineapple, apricot, orange sections; *butter mints; pound cake* pieces; *marshmallows; small cookies; graham cracker* pieces. The fun is having to take more and more bites to decide which way you like it best. Use leftovers (if any) as ice cream topping. If you don't have a fondue pot heat on stove over medium low heat, then place on table over warming candle. But you might want to consider investing in a fondue pot—there seems to be a very special togetherness about crowding around a big pot of something yummy to eat.

Activities

Table games, jigsaw puzzles, and reading aloud are good family night activities. In our family, charades are the classic favorites. Dragging out the old family movies that you haven't seen in years can be a scream. To avoid the "parents have to plan and the kids always complain" syndrome, take turns planning activities (we go from oldest to youngest). That way the parents get a turn to complain, too. The person doing the planning gives a *short* devotional, too—often no more than quoting a favorite Bible verse and leading in prayer, but it's good training for assuming spiritual leadership in their own homes someday.

7

LUNCHBOX FAVORITES

Early Morning Rush

"Mom, my zipper's stuck on my coat."

"Okay, hand me the soap."

"Don't worry about the jelly on my face, my zipper's . . ."

"I heard you. Give me the soap." (Runs soap over the zipper.) "See?"

"Wow! Where'd you learn that?"

"From my daddy—he was a plumber."

"Our teacher uses pencil lead sometimes."

"Soap for plumbers and pencil lead for teachers—makes sense."

"What do moms use?"

"Spit."

"Spit? Yuck!"

"Sure, haven't you ever seen me press Elizabeth's ribbons by licking them and running them through my fingers?"

"Yeah, I guess so. Where'd you learn that?"

"From my mother. And she from hers, I suppose. I think that's what the Bible means about 'One generation passes unto the next and the sun also rises.' "

"What are you talking about?"

"I don't know—but if you don't leave now you'll be late for school. Got your lunch?"

"Yeah. Bye." (slam)

"Wait, you've got jelly on your fa . . . Oh well."

Flaky Cookies

In a big bowl beat together 2 cubes *margarine*, 1 cup *brown sugar* and 1 cup *white sugar*. Add 2 *eggs*. Stir in 2 cups *coconut*, 2 cups *flaked cereal* (Wheaties are good), 2½ cups *flour*, ½ teaspoon *baking powder*, 1 teaspoon *soda*, and ½ teaspoon *vanilla*.

Roll in balls the size of a walnut and bake at 350° for 10 minutes.

Pound Cookies

Cook 2 cups of *quick oatmeal* for 10 minutes in 1 cup *margarine*. Let cool.

Simmer 1 pound of *raisins* 15 minutes in water to cover. Drain.

Mix together: *Oatmeal, raisins*, 2 *eggs*, 1 cup *sugar*, ⅓ cup *milk*, 1 teaspoon *soda*, 2 cups *flour*, 1 pound chopped *dates*, and 1 cup *walnut pieces*.

Drop on cookie sheet by teaspoonfuls. Bake at 350° for 15 minutes.

Jiffy Peanut Butter Cookies

Cut 1 cup *crunchy peanut butter* and 1 cube *margarine* into 1 box *yellow cake mix* using low speed of electric mixer. Add 2 *eggs* and 2 tablespoons *water*. Mix well.

Shape into golf ball sizes and flatten on cookie sheet with tines of a fork. Bake at 350° for 10-12 minutes.

Or, make holes in center of each ball with thumb, and fill with *jelly* immediately after taking out of oven.

Next time, put a *chocolate kiss* in the center of each one before baking.

Applesaucy Cookies

Simmer 2 cups *raisins* 15 or 20 minutes in water to cover. Drain. (I do this for all recipes calling for raisins—try it; you won't believe how much difference it makes!)

Mix together: 1 cup *margarine*, 2 cups *sugar*, 2 *eggs*, 2 cups *applesauce*, 2 teaspoons *soda*, 4 cups *flour* (sift it if you didn't buy pre-sifted), ½ teaspoon *salt*, 1 teaspoon *nutmeg*, 1 teaspoon *cinnamon*, ½ teaspoon *cloves*, and the *raisins*.

Drop by small spoonfuls on cookie sheet and bake at 375° for 10 minutes.

Pumpkin Cookies

Mix together: ½ cup *margarine*, 1 *egg*, 1 cup *sugar*, 1 cup *pumpkin*, 2¼ cups *flour*, 2 teaspoons *baking powder*, 1 teaspoon *cinnamon*, ¼ teaspoon *ginger*, ¼ teaspoon *nutmeg*, ½ teaspoon *salt*, ½ teaspoon *vanilla*, 1 cup *raisins* (simmered as above), ½ cup *walnut pieces*.

Drop by teaspoons and bake 12 minutes at 350°.

The morning after Halloween bake your Jack-o-lanterns (about 20 minutes at 350°), cut off peelings, beat the pulp to a pulp, and freeze it in small containers. This will keep you supplied until next Halloween.

Raisin-filled Cookies

Cream: ½ cup *margarine,* 1 cup *sugar,* 1 *egg.* Stir in: 3¼ cups *flour,* ½ teaspoon *soda,* 1 teaspoon *baking powder,* ½ teaspoon *salt,* ½ teaspoon *vanilla,* ½ cup *sour cream.* Chill dough 1 hour.

Prepare filling: Cook 1½ cups finely cut *raisins,* ½ cup *sugar,* ½ cup *water,* and 2 tablespoons *lemon juice* until slightly thickened, stirring constantly.

Roll dough ¼'' thick. Cut with sugar—cookie cutter or empty tuna can. Place a teaspoon of filling in center of one round piece of dough. Moisten edges with water, and place another round on top. Pinch edges together *very* well. Bake at 375° for 8 minutes until just barely brown.

If you're expecting a chapter on Lunchbox Favorites to include creative sandwich fillings—grated *carrots* in the *tuna fish* and *apples* and *raisins* in the *peanut butter*—forget it. My kids would think they had been poisoned by anything other than good old cheese and mayo or peanut butter and jelly. And what's even more humiliating, they wouldn't be able to find anybody to trade it off on! So save the *creamed cheese* and *chopped olives* with *tuna* and *alfalfa sprouts,* or banana and *apple* slices with *peanut butter* on toasted *raisin bread* for the ladies fellowship.

8

A POT OF TEA JUST FOR ME

Psalm 107

Then they cried out to the Lord in their trouble,
And he brought them out of their distress.
He stilled the storm to a whisper,
The waves of the sea were hushed.
They were glad when it grew calm,
And he guided them to their desired haven.
                              (Psalm 107:29-31 NIV)

Dinner to fix and the baby is crying—she hasn't
    slept well today—probably teething.
Needs her pants changed too.
Dad wants it quiet so he can work.
Phone rings.
Mother is the calm at the center of the storm.

Preston comes in crying—a bad day at school,
Someone called him a name—or he called
    someone—
They punched it out.
Stew is scorching.
Doorbell rings.
Mother is the calm at the center of the storm.

John fell against the hearth—his head is
   bleeding—
Heads bleed like crazy.
He's screaming and crying—
Is he more hurt or scared?
Get a wet towel and some ice (forget about
   the blood on the carpet).
Mother is the calm at the center of the storm.

Stanley needs help with his homework—
Test tomorrow and he left his book at school.
Time to put the baby to bed.
I told my husband we could have time to talk
   this evening.
Dinner dishes still not done.
Stanley needs laundry done for tomorrow,
And there's still the homework.
Mother is the calm at the center of the storm.

But who is the calm at the center of my storm?
"Lord, be my calm."
My little ship is tossed and buffeted and
   sometimes I fear the waves.
"He rebuked the wind and said to the waves,
   'Quiet! Be still!'
Then the wind died down and it was completely
   calm."

Tea Making

Tea making expertise: There are 3 absolutely
nonnegotiable rules for making a good pot of tea:
1. The tea, whatever flavor or blend, must be of a
good quality; 2. The water must be at a full, rolling boil; 3. The tea must steep for 3 to 5 minutes

until the tea leaves sink to the bottom of the pot.

I'm less adamant about the remaining rules: 1. Preheat the pot by filling it with hot tap water and dumping out before putting in the tea; 2. Use a cozy to cover a pot that must sit for awhile; 3. Use loose tea, not bags. Put straight in the pot and pour out through a strainer (good English china tea pots are made with tiny holes at the base of the sprout); 4. For proper English tea use 1 teaspoon tea per cup. For American tastes, 1 heaping teaspoon tea per pot; 5. English Breakfast and English Tea Time blends should be served strong with milk and sugar. Earl Gray should be drunk straight, just as it comes from the pot. Herbal blends are great, but not for a real tea party; 6. A pot of tea just for me is a lovely luxury, but it's even nicer when shared with a friend, and nicest of all if the friend has a little girl to bring with her. In summer set the tea table on the grass.

Strawberry Dips

The nicest way to serve fresh strawberries is whole, with even the stems on to serve as handles when berries are dipped into something sweet and wonderful, such as: *Powdered sugar;* or 1 cup *sour cream* mixed with ¼ cup *brown sugar;* or my favorite, *Almond Chantilly:* Prepare 1 small package *instant vanilla pudding mix* according to package directions. Fold in 1 teaspoon *almond extract* and 1 cup *heavy cream,* whipped.

Tea Sandwiches

Cut slices of *white bread* into fun shapes with cookie cutters. Spread with soft *butter.* Slice a *cucumber* and several *radishes.* Top sandwiches with 1 slice of cucumber or 3 overlapping slices of radish. Garnish with bits of *parsley.*

Trim crusts off slices of *white bread,* spread thinly with soft *butter,* then *mayonnaise.* Drain well 1 can *asparagus spears.* Place a stalk of asparagus at end of slice and roll up. Wrap rolls tightly in dampened cloth and refrigerate until tea time.

Tea Cookies

Shortbread: Mix 3 cups *flour,* ¾ cup *butter,* 2 *egg yolks* (save egg whites for another recipe), and 1 cup *sugar* until a soft dough forms. Chill. Roll ½'' thick. Cut in triangles. Sprinkle with *sugar* and bake at 375° for 8 minutes. Don't brown.

Pecan Drops: Cream ½ cup *butter* and ½ cup plus 2 tablespoons *shortening.* Mix in 2½ cups *cake flour,* 2 teaspoons *vanilla,* and 1 cup finely chopped *pecans.* Drop by small teaspoonfuls on cookie sheet. Bake at 325° for 6-8 minutes until barely browned. Roll in *powdered sugar* immediately. Store in a tight jar.

Lemon Bars: Cut 1 cup *butter* into 2 cups *flour* and ½ cup *powdered sugar.* When crumbly, pat into a 9'' x 13'' pan and bake 20 minutes at 350°. Brown only very lightly.

While crust bakes, beat 4 *eggs,* 4 tablespoons *flour,* 2 cups *sugar,* and the juice and grated rind of 2 *lemons.* Pour over hot crust and bake 20 minutes. Cool and sift *powdered sugar* over the top. Cut in small rectangles. If hard to cut, dip knife in hot water.

9
HAPPY FOOD

The Happy Book

"I hate school.

"I hate playing the recorder.

"I hate ... ."

"Whoa. Look, honey, you can choose whether to be happy or unhappy. About an equal number of good and bad things happen every day; you just have to decide which you're going to pay most attention to.

"Let's try something. Everyday at bedtime we'll write one happy thing that happened that day in this notebook. When we have 30 things, I'll take you out for a doughnut."

"Okay. That's the good thing for today."

Rainbow Cake

This cake has 4 layers, top to bottom: White, pink, yellow, chocolate. You will need 1 box *loaf-size white cake mix* and 1 box *loaf-size yellow cake mix*.

Prepare white mix according to package directions, adding 3 tablespoons *margarine* and 1 teaspoon *vanilla* to ingredients. Divide batter in half; to one half add 2 drops *red food coloring*. Bake in 8'' cake pans at 350° for 12-15 minutes.

Prepare yellow cake mix, adding 3 tablespoons *margarine* and 1 teaspoon *vanilla* to package directions. Divide batter in half; to one half add 1 square *unsweetened chocolate* melted with 1 tablespoon *milk*. To remaining batter add 5 drops *yellow food coloring*. Bake in 8'' pans, at 350° for 12-15 minutes.

When layers are cool frost between layers and all over outside with *7-Minute Frosting:*

In top of double boiler place 3 *egg whites*, 2 cups *sugar*, 3 teaspoons *light corn syrup*, ½ cup cold *water*, a dash of *salt*. Beat 1 minute, then place over boiling water and cook, beating constantly for 7 minutes. Remove from heat. Add 1 teaspoon *vanilla*. Beat 2 minutes more.

Of course, a mix will work, too—but this is better.

Smile Cookies

Cream 1½ cups *sugar* with 1 cup *margarine*. Beat in 2 *eggs*. Stir in 3 cups *flour*, ½ teaspoon *soda*, ½ teaspoon *salt* alternately with 3 tablespoons *sour cream* and ¼ teaspoon *vanilla*.

Chill dough well. Roll as thin as a dime. Cut out with a tuna fish can that has both top and bottom removed. Bake 6 minutes at 375°. You don't want them to brown.

I have a friend who rolls her sugar cookie dough into little balls and flattens the balls with the bottom of a glass right on the cookie tray. It's speedy and fun for small children, but the shapes aren't as nice.

For an even faster approach, buy 2 packages of plain sugar cookies.

For icing, cream 1 box *powdered sugar*, 4 tablespoons *margarine* (whipped diet margarine makes a nice, light frosting), 1 tablespoon *lemon juice*, 2 tablespoons *milk*, and a few drops *yellow food coloring*. Spread on cookies. (Add more milk if icing doesn't spread smoothly.)

Make smiles with 2½" pieces of *rope licorice* and eyes with *chocolate chips*.

Surprise Cookies

Cream together: 1 cup *margarine*, 1 cup *sugar*, ½ cup *brown sugar*, 2 *eggs*, 1 tablespoon *water*, and 1 teaspoon *vanilla*. Stir in: 3 cups *flour*, 1 teaspoon *soda*, ½ teaspoon *salt*. Refrigerate 2 hours.

Place a small, *mint-flavored chocolate wafer* in 1 tablespoon dough and fold dough around completely. Bake at 375° for 10 minutes. Each cookie may be topped with a *pecan* or *walnut piece* before baking also.

Peanut Butter and Jelly Muffins

Combine 2 cups *flour*, ½ cup *sugar*, 2½ teaspoons *baking powder*, and ½ teaspoon *salt*. Cut in ¾ cup *crunchy peanut butter* with fork. Add ¾ cup *milk* and 2 *eggs*. Stir just to moisten dough.

Place 2 tablespoons batter in greased muffin cup. Place 1 teaspoon *jelly* in center, then top with 2 tablespoons more batter. Bake at 400° for 15 minutes.

10
COME OVER FOR COFFEE

Coffee With Joan

"Donna, what's the thing in your life that has caused you to grow most, spiritually? I'm sort of taking a survey."

Long, thinking pause.

"Answered prayer. Because when things get tough, I can look back to the high points and hold on to them—like biblical promises."

"That's neat! I like that! Most people say 'the death of a loved one,' or 'my surgery,' until you get the idea you can't grow spiritually if things are going well. Makes you feel guilty."

"I know what you mean. That's like with our children, too. They need to know what they're doing right just as much as what they're doing wrong—they grow from both."

Fruit Cocktail Torte
Dump together: a 303 can of *fruit cocktail* with juice, 1 cup *sugar*, 1 cup *flour*, ½ teaspoon *salt*, 1

teaspoon *soda,* 1 *egg.* Stir and pour into 8" x 8" greased pan.

Sprinkle ½ cup *dark brown sugar* and ½ cup *chopped walnuts* on top. Bake 50 minutes at 350°. Serve with *whipped cream.*

Coffee With Saundra
(mother of 9½ children)

"Saundra, my doctor is bugging me about getting Elizabeth to sleep through the night. Now when I get up with her I feel guilty, and when I don't she wakens the rest of the family and then I *really* feel guilty. What do you do?"

"I get up with them. You know, you don't really lose that much sleep and sometimes that's the only time I have in the whole day to be alone with that baby and cuddle it. But you can spoil them. You've got to decide whether an older baby is really hungry or just working Mama. I did that with Travis. He was getting me up at 5:30 every morning for a playtime. It was *my* fault, but *he* had to suffer for it when it came time that we had to cry it out.

"I lay in the next room listening to him and cried right along with him. But you know, the Lord showed me something really special— Travis didn't know I was in the next room suffering with him, but I was. Sometimes I don't know where God is when I have a problem, but he's right in the next room crying with me."

"Saundra, that's beautiful! You should write about that."

"And when do you think I'd have the time?"

Cranberry Crunch

Mix 1 cup *oatmeal*, ½ cup *flour*, 1 cup *brown sugar*, and ½ cup *butter* until crumbly. Spread half of the mixture on the bottom of a greased 8'' x 8'' pan. Spread with a small can of *cranberry sauce* (jellied or whole berry). Top with rest of crumbly. Bake 35 minutes at 325°.

A scoop of *vanilla ice cream* on top is yummy, too, when the Cranberry Crunch is served warm.

Coffee With Barbara

"How is Bobby liking his new class, Barbara?"

"Mmmm, got a problem. There are some girls in there that are really quick with their work and Bobby likes to take his time. They tell him he's stupid and he believes it."

"But Bobby is so bright—that's awful!"

"I know. Yesterday he told me he was stupid and I said, 'Bobby, you're green.' His mouth fell open and he said, 'What?' 'You're green.' 'No I'm not.' 'Well, then, does having somebody say you're stupid make it true any more than saying you're green makes you green?' "

Apple Pan Cake

Spread 1 can *apple pie filling* in 9'' x 13'' pan. Sprinkle 2 cups *flour*, 1 cup *sugar*, 1½ teaspoons *soda* and ½ teaspoon *salt* over apples. Mix 2 *eggs*, 1 teaspoon *vanilla* and ⅔ cup *cooking oil;* pour over dry ingredients. Stir lightly. Top with ½ cup *walnut bits*. Bake at 350° for 40 minutes.

While cake bakes combine 1 cup *sugar*, 1 cup *sour cream*, and ½ teaspoon *soda* in small saucepan. Cook and stir over medium heat until mixture comes to a boil.

When cake is done, prick with a fork and pour hot topping over it.

Coffee With Sue

She's sure to be on a diet, but I'll make a cake anyway—that's why she's a size 8 and I'm a size 12.

Lemon Glaze Cake

Beat one package *lemon cake mix* with 4 *eggs*, ¾ cup *water*, ⅔ cup *oil*, and one package *lemon jello*. Pour in a 9″ x 13″ pan and bake 30 minutes at 350°.

Have ¼ cup *lemon juice* and 1½ cups *powdered sugar* warm when cake comes out of oven. Prick cake with fork and drizzle lemon glaze over it.

Iced Coffee

Dissolve 6 heaping teaspoons *decaffeinated instant coffee* and ¼ cup *sugar* in 1 cup *boiling water.* Let cool. At serving time add 1 quart cold *milk* and a dash of *nutmeg* or *cinnamon.*

(For dieting friends use 9 *saccahrin tablets* in place of sugar and *skim milk.*)

11
FOOD FOR GIFTS

Christmas Letter

"I have written no books yet, gone on no trips to Europe, Hawaii, or even California, run for no political office, been involved in no scandalous affairs, had no babies nor serious illnesses, and unless you wish to read of gardening, canning, cooking, church involvement, swimming lessons, and endless hours of cleaning house, it seems I have done nothing of sufficient interest to take space in this letter. I am, however, happy and healthy and truly delighted to be spending Christmas with my beloved little family."

Love,
Lana

These are especially nice for children to make—supervised, of course. That way they can have the fun of making them and giving them to teachers, grandmas, and aunts as their very own gifts.

For containers, collect a number of *small jars* (baby food, junior food, jelly, etc). Remove the lids and cover them with craft dough: Mix 2 cups *flour*, 1 cup *salt* and 1 cup *water* to a soft dough. Knead smooth. Take a golf ball sized piece of dough and flatten with palm of hand. Cup over lid. Score with table knife to resemble a mushroom cap.

Place lids on foil-covered cookie sheet and bake at 325° for 1 hour or until lightly browned. When cool, finish with a coat of *shellac* and glue a little arrangement of *hard candies, dried beans, sunflower seeds,* etc. to top. When jar is filled, tie a *bow* around its neck just under the lid.

And what to put inside? Just fill with the same candies that decorate the top or choose from the following recipes. I think the teas were the most popular we ever did.

Gift Teas

Spicy Green: Mix 1 cup *green tea* leaves with ½ teaspoon *ground cloves*, 2 tablespoons *grated orange peel*, and ½ teaspoon *ground ginger*.

Anise Alfalfa: Put 2 tablespoons *anise seeds* in a plastic bag and let the kids crush them with a hammer. Mix anise with ½ cup *alfalfa leaves* and ½ cup dried *rose hips.* You may need to go to the health food store for some of these ingredients.

Floral Tea: Combine 1 cup dried *Hibiscus flowers* with ¼ cup *chamomile*.

Mint Cooler: Mix ¼ pound *Darjeeling tea* with ¼ cup *peppermint leaves.*

Cooler than Ever: Mix ¼ pound *mint tea* with ¼ cup *eucalyptus leaves.*

Spicy Orange: Put 5 *cinnamon sticks* and 2½

tablespoons *whole cloves* in a plastic bag and let the kids go at them with a hammer again. Mix spices with ¼ pound *orange pekoe tea*, ¼ cup *dried orange peel*, ¼ cup finely chopped *candied ginger*, and 1 teaspoon *ground nutmeg*.

Mocha Mix: Mix 1 cup *nondairy creamer*, 1 cup *cocoa mix*, ⅔ cup *instant coffee powder*, ½ cup *sugar*, ½ teaspoon *ground cinnamon*, ¼ teaspoon *ground nutmeg*.

Flavored Butters

Don't let these sit under the Christmas tree. Keep refrigerated until gift-giving time.

Honey Butter: See chapter 5.

Onion Butter: Mix ½ cup *butter*, ¼ cup snipped fresh *parsley*, ¼ cup minced *onion*, 2 teaspoons *Worcestershire sauce*, ½ teaspoon dry *mustard*, and ½ teaspoon freshly ground *pepper*. Beat. Great for flavoring broiled meats.

Orange Butter: Combine ½ cup *butter*, 2 table-spoons *grated orange peel*, ½ teaspoon *ground coriander*, ½ teaspoon *ginger*. Beat. Try it on toasted raisin bread.

Sesame Seed Butter: Place 2 tablespoons sesame seeds on a pie pan in a 325° oven for 5-8 minutes until golden. Beat with ½ cup *butter* and ½ teaspoon *garlic powder*. Recommended for French bread.

Chili Garlic Butter: Beat ½ cup *butter* with 1 teaspoon *chili powder*, 1 clove finely minced *garlic*, ¼ teaspoon *ground cumin*. Try it on hot vegetables.

Glazed Nuts

Spiced Walnuts: Combine 1 cup *sugar*, ½ teaspoon *nutmeg*, 1/8 teaspoon *cream of tartar*, ¼ cup boiling *water*. Cook to 240° (soft ball stage) on a candy thermometer. Stir in ½ teaspoon *vanilla* and 2 cups *walnuts*. Spread out on waxed paper to cool.

Orange Glazed Nuts: Cook 1½ cups *sugar*, ¼ cup *water*, and 3 tablespoons *orange juice* to 240° on candy thermometer (soft ball). Stir in 1 tablespoon *grated orange rind* and ½ pound assorted *nuts*—pecans, almonds, walnuts. Keep stirring until glaze crystallizes. Spread on waxed paper and separate nuts.

Cheese Spreads

These should be refrigerated until given, but let stand at room temperature before serving.

Cheddar Spread: Grate 1 pound of *sharp cheddar cheese* into a mixing bowl. Add 2 tablespoons soft *butter*, 1 teaspoon *Dijon mustard*, 2 teaspoons *brandy flavoring*, 1/8 teaspoon *basil*, a pinch of *dill weed*, and ½ teaspoon *paprika*. Blend well. This makes 3 cups so you can fill several small jars. Serve on rye krisp or melba toast.

Creamy Olive Nut Spread: Blend together well 8 ounces *cream cheese*, ¼ cup *butter*, ½ teaspoon *salt*, 1 small can *chopped olives*, ½ cup finely chopped *walnuts*. Serve on whole wheat crackers.

Ham and Cheese Spread: Beat 2 8-ounce packages *cream cheese* and 1 cup grated *cheddar cheese* and 1 cup grated *Swiss cheese* until fluffy. Add 2 teaspoons *onion powder*, 2 teaspoons *Worcestershire sauce*, 1 teaspoon *season salt*, ½ teaspoon *salt*, ½ teaspoon *paprika*, and 1 (2½-ounce) can *deviled ham*. Mix well.

Play Dough

And for the children on your gift list or your own children on a rainy day no frantic mother should be without a really good playdough recipe. Here it is!

Dissolve 1 tablespoon *alum* in 2 cups *boiling water*. Stir in 2 cups *flour*, 3 tablespoons *vegetable oil* and desired *food coloring*. Knead in about ½ cup more *flour* by hand to form soft, workable dough. This will keep for ages *if* stored in an air tight container.

12
MEMORY COOKIES

Old Age Insurance

We made decorations for the Christmas tree—
  We made memories.

We made a batch of decorated cookies—
  We made memories.

We made gifts for the neighbors—
  We made memories.

We made a snowman—
  We made memories.

When they are far away with children of their
  own, Making their own memories,
They'll have these memories to keep with them.
And we will too.

Decorated Sugar Cookies
This is my favorite childhood Christmas tradi-
tion memory. Mother and I always spent a whole

day at it—our results were works of art. Then we spent another day calling on special friends and leaving plates of our treasures.

For a simplified version of our project, prepare a batch of the *Smile Cookies* from chapter 9, cutting with an empty tuna can. Then cut a smaller, 1" diameter circle from center to make wreaths. Bake and cool.

Mix 1 box *powdered sugar*, 1 teaspoon *vanilla*, 2 tablespoons *butter*, and 3 tablespoons *milk*. Put about ¼ cup icing in a small bowl and tint with red *food coloring*. Put about ⅓ cup icing in another bowl and tint with green *food coloring*. Put red icing in cake decorator with writing tip and green icing in cake decorator with leaf tip. Spread white icing on wreaths. (White icing may need a few drops more milk to spread smoothly.) Make 3 groups of leaves (2 or 3 leaves per group) around wreath. Put 2 or 3 red berries on leaves and make a red bow with cake decorator.

(Or you can buy tubes of red gel and green icing with decorator tips. These are easier for smaller children to handle.)

Holly
Melt 30 *marshmallows* with 1 cube *margarine*. Stir in 1 teaspoon *green food coloring*, 1 teaspoon *vanilla*, and 4 cups *corn flakes*. Drop on waxed paper. Decorate with *red hot candy "berries."*

Frost Balls
Combine ¾ cup *butter*, 1 teaspoon *vanilla*, 1 tablespoon *water*, 1/8 teaspoon *salt* and ⅓ cup *sugar*. Stir in 2 cups sifted *cake flour* and 1 (6-oz.) package *chocolate chips*. Shape into 1" balls and bake on ungreased cookie sheet for 30 minutes at

300°. Roll in *white sugar* while still warm.

Gingerbread Men

Combine 1 package *gingerbread mix*, ½ cup *water*, ⅓ cup *flour*, and 2 tablespoons *margarine*. Chill 2 hours. Roll ¼" thick and cut with gingerbread man cookie cutter. Bake 10 minutes at 350°.

Make *white icing* from sugar cookie recipe above. Pipe on clothing outlines and facial features, or use icing to stick on *raisin* eyes and buttons. Pipe bows in hair to make some girls. Buy *miniature candy canes for some to carry.*

Oh, Dolly, Oh!

Melt 1 cube *butter* or *margarine* in a 9" x 13" pan. Add: 1 cup *graham cracker crumbs*, 1 cup *coconut*, 1 cup *chocolate chips*, 1 cup *butterscotch chips*, 1 cup chopped *nuts*, 1 can *sweetened condensed milk*. Run knife through to mix a bit. Bake at 325° for half an hour.

Rocky Road Bars

Melt together 1 cube *margarine* and 1 square *unsweetened chocolate*. Mix well with: 1 cup *sugar*, 1 cup *flour*, ½ cup chopped *nuts*, 1 teaspoon *baking powder*, 1 teaspoon *vanilla*, 2 *eggs*. Spread in greased 9" x 13" pan.

Combine: 6 ounces *cream cheese* (from an 8-oz. package), ½ cup *sugar*, 2 tablespoons *flour*, ½ cup *margarine*, 1 *egg*, and ½ teaspoon *vanilla*. Spread over layer in pan. Sprinkle with ¼ cup chopped *nuts* and 1 package (6-oz.) *chocolate chips*. Bake 30 minutes at 350° until toothpick inserted in center comes out clean. Sprinkle with 2 cups *miniature marshmallows* and bake 2 minutes longer.

Melt together over low heat: ¼ cup *margarine*, 1 ounce *unsweetened chocolate*, reserved *cream cheese*, ¼ cup *milk*. Stir in 1 box *powdered sugar* and 1 teaspoon *vanilla*. Beat smooth and pour over marshmallows and swirl together.

Cut into 3 dozen small bars. They are incredibly rich.

Butterscotch Drops

Cream ½ cup plus 2 tablespoons *butter* with 1½ cups *brown sugar* and 2 *eggs*. Stir in 2½ cups *flour*, ½ teaspoon *baking powder*, 1 teaspoon *soda*, and ¼ teaspoon *salt* alternately with 1 cup *sour cream* (naturally soured whipping cream is even better than commercial sour cream).

Stir in 1 teaspoon *vanilla* and ⅔ cup chopped *nuts*. Drop by teaspoonfuls on greased cookie sheet about 3 inches apart. Bake 10 minutes at 350°.

Frost with *Burnt Butter Icing:* Melt 6 tablespoons *butter* until lightly browned. Stir in 1½ cups *powdered sugar*, 1 teaspoon *vanilla* and 2 tablespoons *hot water*. Beat until of spreading consistency.

Popcorn Balls

Pop 2 or more poppers of popcorn. This will equal about 8 quarts *popcorn*.

Combine *1 cup sugar*, ¼ cup *butter* or *margarine*, ⅓ cup *white corn syrup*, ⅓ cup *water*, and ¾ teaspoon *salt* in heavy saucepan. Stir over medium high heat until sugar dissolves. Cook to hard ball stage (270°). Stir in 1 teaspoon *vanilla*. Pour over popped corn in large pan. Rub margarine on hands and form into balls, being careful not to burn fingers.

13
RÉCHAUFFÉ

Bible Study Feedback

"What did you think of that film on the Second Coming?"

"Awesome."

"If they have the rapture, Mama will have to nurse Elizabeth on the way up."

"What's for dinner?"

"Well, speaking of second coming—leftovers."

"Oooooh, that was pretty bad."

"Leftovers. Yuck!"

"Preston, don't say yuck to your mother's cooking."

"We'll call it réchauffé and think of it as French."

"French food?! *YUCK!*"

"Preston, I just said . . ."

Beef in Cream

Combine ¼ cup *margarine*, 1 cup *heavy cream*, 1 clove minced *garlic*, 2 tablespoons *lemon juice*,

¾ teaspoon *salt,* ¼ teaspoon *pepper.* Heat until butter melts. Pour half of sauce in casserole, top with slices of *leftover roast beef,* pour rest of sauce over top, and bake at 350° for 15 minutes.

Chicken or Turkey Chow Mein
Sauté 1½ cups chopped *celery,* 1 chopped green *pepper,* and 1 can sliced *water chestnuts* in 3 tablespoons *margarine.* Add 3 cups *leftover chicken* or *turkey* cubes (or however much you have), ½ cup *soy sauce,* ⅓ cup *water,* and 1 can *pineapple pie filling.* Heat together and serve over *rice* or *chow mein noodles.*

Saucy Ham Strips
Sauté strips of *leftover ham* (about 1 cup) and ½ cup chopped *onion* in 2 tablespoons *margarine.* Stir in 2 tablespoons *flour,* 1 cup *sour cream,* and 1 small can sliced *black olives.* Cook and stir 3 or 4 minutes until thickened. Serve over *buttered toast* or *biscuits.*

Egg Casserole
Use this one the day after Easter—my kids think I'm awful because I make them store their Easter eggs in the refrigerator, and what's worse, I won't let them have egg wars.

Fill a 2-quart casserole with layers of sliced *hard-boiled eggs,* diced *ham* or *tuna,* and sliced *mushrooms* (if desired). In a small saucepan, combine 1 can *cream of celery soup,* ½ cup *milk,* 2 cups grated *sharp cheddar cheese,* 2 teaspoons *Worcestershire sauce,* a few drops *Tabasco sauce.* Cook and stir until cheese melts. Pour over top of casserole.

Toast 2 slices *whole wheat bread* until crisp. Tear into crumbs. Toss with 3 tablespoons melted *margarine*. Sprinkle over casserole. Bake at 350° for 30 minutes.

Vegetable Beef Soup

Nutritionists tell us we'd be better off if we threw away the vegetables and drank the cooking water. Here's how to get the best of both.

Collect the water in which you boil vegetables, or over which you steam them until you have 2 quarts. Also save leftover vegetables in coldest part of refrigerator or freezer.

Combine in soup kettle: 1 can *tomato puree*, 1 minced clove *garlic*, 1 chopped *onion*, 1 chopped *celery* stalk, 1 diced *carrot*, 1 diced *potato*, 2 teaspoons *salt*, ¼ teaspoon *pepper*. Simmer 10 minutes.

Add 2 quarts *vegetable water* and 2 teaspoons *beef bouillon* and bring to a boil. Drop 1 pound *hamburger*, in bits, into boiling broth. Cook 5-7 minutes. Add *leftover vegetables* (thawed) and heat through.

Sugar Cube Biscuits

Use these to sweeten the taste of leftovers. Place 1 can *refrigerator buttermilk biscuits* in a well-buttered pan. For each biscuit dip a *sugar cube* in *orange juice* and press into center of dough. Bake at 400° for 12 minutes. Serve with *butter*. M-m-m-m!

or

Cheese Biscuits

Place ½ teaspoon *margarine* and 1 tablespoon shredded *cheese* (any kind) in each of 10 muffin cups. Top with *refrigerator dough biscuits*. Bake 10 minutes at 400°.

14

AFTER CHURCH BRUNCH

Outreach

"Do you realize we're probably the only three Christian families in this whole subdivision?"

"I know. I'd love to do some outreach, but I'm not much on knocking on doors."

"So let's get them over to knock on ours."

"What do you mean?"

"How about a neighborhood Sunday brunch? Invite them to go to church with us first, if they want, but it's not required."

"Great! Next Sunday there's a special musician at church. Maybe he'd come too. Maybe he'd even sing for us! Wow!"

"So what do we serve?"

"How about my friend the fritatta?"

"The what?"

"Fritatta. It's a kind of Italian omelette."

"Uh-oh, bet it's hard to do."

"Bet you're wrong."

Cheese Fritatta

Beat 6 *eggs* with 1 teaspoon *salt* and 1 teaspoon *sugar*. Cut 1 pound *jack cheese* and 12 ounces *cream cheese* into small cubes, stir into egg mixture with 1 cup *cottage cheese* and 1 tablespoon *butter*. Stir in 1 teaspoon *baking powder* and ½ cup *flour*.

Bake in a 9'' x 13'' pan for 40 minutes at 350°. Cut into squares to serve.

Artichoke Fritatta

Beat 6 *eggs*. Stir in 3 undrained jars *marinated artichoke hearts,* sliced, 10 *soda crackers,* crushed, and ½ pound *sharp cheddar cheese,* grated.

Bake in a 9'' x 13'' pan for 30 minutes at 350°. Cut in squares to serve.

Browned Onion Fritatta

Chop 2 medium *onions* and cook in 1 tablespoon *oil* until well browned, about 15 minutes over medium low heat.

Beat 4 *eggs,* 2 tablespoons *milk,* ¼ cup *parmesan cheese,* and a dash of *pepper.* Heat 1 teaspoon *oil* in an 8'' skillet and pour in egg mixture. Cook over low heat until eggs are set and golden brown on bottom. Sprinkle with browned onion; broil until eggs are set on top, about 2 minutes. Cut in wedges to serve.

And to Drink

Offer an assortment of chilled juices: *Sparkling white* and *red grape juices; orange juice, apple juice,* and *cranberry juice* are all delicious mixed with equal parts *7-Up; apricot nectar* is exotic; and *tomato juice spiced with lemon juice, salt, horseradish,* and *Worcestershire sauce* to taste is zingy.

Coffee Cake Quickies

Date Mix Cake: Prepare filling and crumb mixture for a 14-ounce box of *date bar mix* according to package directions. Pat 1½ cups of the crumb mixture in 9'' x 9'' baking pan.

Combine 2 cups *biscuit mix,* 3 tablespoons *sugar,* ⅔ cup *milk,* 1 *egg,* and 2 tablespoons *oil.* Spread half this mixture over crumbs in pan, spread date filling over this, then more biscuit mixture and sprinkle with remaining crumbs. Bake at 375° for 35 minutes or until toothpick inserted in center comes out clean.

Orange Ring Mold: Make a thick syrup by cooking 1 cube *butter* with 1½ cups *brown sugar.* Pour half the syrup in the bottom of a large ring mold. Sprinkle with ½ cup *pecan bits.* Slant 2 packages *refrigerator biscuits* around mold. Drain well 1 can *mandarin oranges* and 1 small can *pineapple chunks.* Push fruit pieces in between biscuits. Pour rest of syrup over top. Bake 25-30 minutes at 400°.

Cranberry Bubble Loaf: Combine 2 *biscuit mix* and ½ cup *orange juice.* Divide dough into 16 portions. Divide a 4-oz. can of *jellied cranberry sauce* into 16 pieces and shape a piece of dough around each piece of cranberry sauce. Roll balls in 4 tablespoons melted *margarine* and dip in ½ cup *brown sugar* mixed with 1 teaspoon *grated orange peel.* Place in loaf pan and bake 30 minutes at 350°.

Let stand 5 minutes, then remove from pan

and roast with a mixture of ½ cup *powdered sugar*, 2 teaspoons *milk*, and ½ teaspoon *vanilla*.

Baked Ambrosia

Drain well: (1 can each) *Apricot halves, peach halves, purple plums, pineapple slices.* Slice one *orange* thin. Arrange fruit in large baking dish. Mix ½ cup *orange juice*, ¼ cup *brown sugar*, ½ tablespoon *lemon peel*, 2 tablespoons melted *butter*. Pour over fruit. Sprinkle ½ cup *coconut* over all. Bake at 425° for 15 minutes until coconut is toasted. Serve warm.

And if we eat on the deck we can do sausages on the grill. Now, who has a *big* coffee pot?

15
BEDTIME SNACKS

Red-Letter Day

Today?
What did I do today?
I loved my family.

Of course I did a mountain of laundry,
Fixed three meals—about ten times (schedules
   differ so),
Straightened the house—you know how it is.

But those aren't the important things,
Not really.
Mostly I loved my family—
That's what counts.

Cocoa Floats

Break 6 ounces *unsweetened chocolate* into
small pieces in a saucepan. Add 1 quart *milk*, 2
teaspoons *flour* and ½ cup *sugar*. Cook and stir
until chocolate melts and milk *almost* boils.

Lower heat and cook and stir *very slowly* until slightly thick.

Pour into mugs and top each with a small scoop of *vanilla ice cream*.

Cinnamon Toasties

Brush slices of *bread* generously with melted *margarine*. Combine ¼ cup *sugar*, 1 tablespoon *cinnamon*, and 2 tablespoons *powdered sugar* in a large shaker. Sprinkle generously over buttered bread. Broil for a few minutes until bubbly and lightly browned. Cut into triangles.

Baked Custard

Heat 1 quart *milk* until very warm. Remove from heat and beat in 4 *eggs*, ¾ cup *sugar*, 1 teaspoon *vanilla*, and ½ teaspoon *almond extract*. Pour into 1½ quart casserole and sprinkle with a little *nutmeg*. Place in a larger pan of hot water and bake at 325° for 30 minutes. Knife inserted in center should come out clean. Serve warm or cold.

This is my favorite food when I'm nursing. It's especially good when you have to get up in the middle of the night. *Artificial sweetener* can be substituted for half the sugar, I use about 1½ grains saccharine or 24 drops liquid sweetener.

Rocky Road

In top of double boiler place 1 large (12-oz.) and 1 small (6-oz.) package of *chocolate chips*. Cook over hot water until melted. Stir in 3 cups *miniature marshmallows* and ¾ cup coarsely broken *walnuts*. Spread on waxed paper to cool; cut in squares.

No one over 18 will want anything this rich at bedtime—adults can eat an apple.

Fried Cheese

Cut *cheese* (any firm kind—cheddar, colby, Swiss, jack, Mozzarella) in about ½'' x 2'' strips. Roll in *flour*, then dip in beaten *egg* and fine *bread crumbs*. Fry lightly in 2 inches of hot *oil* and drain on paper towel.

Applesauce Bars

Dump 4 *eggs*, 1⅔ cup *sugar*, 1 cup *oil*, 2 cups *applesauce*, 2 cups *flour*, 2 teaspoons *baking powder*, 2 teaspoons *cinnamon*, ½ *teaspoon salt*, and 1 teaspoon *soda* together in a big bowl and mix up well. Pour into a 10'' x 15'' jelly roll pan or broiler pan and bake at 350°for 25 minutes. Cool.

Frost with 3 ounces *cream cheese*, 1 cube *margarine*, 1 teaspoon *vanilla*, and 2 cups *powdered sugar* beaten until fluffy.

Orange Smoothie

Place 1 small can *orange juice concentrate*, 1 cup *milk or* 1 cup plain *yogurt*, 1 cup *water*, 1 teaspoon *vanilla*, ½ cup *sugar*, and 10 *ice cubes* in blender and whirl for 30 seconds.

Makes a good appetizer for luncheon or dinner parties, too.

Orange Balls

Crush a 10-oz. package of *vanilla wafers* to crumbs. Mix with 1 box *powdered sugar*, 1 cube melted *margarine*, and 1 small can *orange juice concentrate.* Shape into balls and roll in *flaked coconut.*

Bedtime snacks are important in our family (and so is brushing teeth afterwards), not only because people are often hungry then and will sleep better on a not-empty stomach, but also because it's such a good time to gather in the kitchen or family room and visit for a few minutes, sharing the events of the day or clearing signals for tomorrow and having a good night prayer together.

16
FAMILY PICNIC

Problem Solving

"But I don't see why I can't go fishing with Scott on Sunday morning. It's just once. Missing Sunday school once won't hurt me."

"Go to a movie on *Sunday?*"

"I know you promised to mow the neighbor's lawn this weekend—so why did you leave it till Sunday?"

"I hate to let these problems become a battle-ground where everyone's ego is at stake. After all, God said, 'Remember the Sabbath Day and keep it holy' long before your parents did. So let's pray about it."

"Pray about it—instead of arguing?!"

"Revolutionary, isn't it?"

"*So what can* we do on Sunday?"

"How about a picnic after church?"

Lemon-Marinated Chicken Wings

Combine 1 package *Italian salad dressing mix,* 3 tablespoons *water,* 2 tablespoons *lemon juice,* 2 tablespoons *cooking oil,* and 1 tablespoon *parmesan cheese.* Pour over 2 pounds *chicken wings* and marinate in refrigerator overnight.

May be cooked at the picnic on charcoal grill for 20 to 30 minutes, turning once; or cook before the picnic by baking on wire rack over shallow baking pan for 30 minutes in a 400° oven, turning once. Serve hot or cold.

Mom's Baked Beans

Fry 3 slices of *bacon,* crisp. Remove bacon and brown 1 small diced *onion* in drippings. Add onions and crumbled bacon to a large can of *pork and beans* and stir in 2 tablespoons *catsup,* ¼ cup *brown sugar,* and ½ teaspoon *mustard.* Bake 30 minutes at 350°.

Shrimp Deviled Eggs

Cut 6 *hard-boiled eggs* in half crosswise*. Place yolks in bowl with ½ cup *mayonnaise,* 2 teaspoons *mustard,* 1 tablespoon *lemon juice,* and 1 can *shrimp* pieces, drained. Mash together well. Fill whites with mixture, mounding deliciously.

*To take on picnic, place filled egg halves in styrofoam egg carton. To serve on a plate, you would cut eggs lengthwise.

Grandpa's Potato Salad

No, Grandpa doesn't make it—Grandma does—Grandpa eats it!

Place 3 cups diced cooked *potatoes* in a bowl.

Toss with 1 teaspoon *sugar* and 1 teaspoon *vinegar*. Let stand at room temperature 20 minutes. Fold in gently ¼ cup finely diced *onion*, 1½ teaspoon *salt*, 1½ teaspoon *celery seed*, ¾ cup *mayonnaise*, and 3 *hard-boiled eggs*, diced. Chill.

Penuche Date Cake

Pour 1 cup *boiling water* over 1¼ cups *chopped dates*. (I know you can buy them chopped, but it's worth the effort to buy dates with seeds and cut your own.) Let cool.

Combine ¼ cup *margarine*, 1 cup *sugar*, 1 *egg*, 1 teaspoon *vanilla*. Beat 5 minutes until very fluffy. With mixer on low speed, add 1¾ cups *flour*, ½ teaspoon *salt*, 1 teaspoon *soda* alternately with date mixture. Blend just until smooth. Add ½ cup chopped *nuts*. Bake in 9" x 13" pan 40-45 minutes at 350°. Toothpick inserted in center should come out clean.

Penuche Icing: Melt ¼ cup *butter* in saucepan. Add ½ cup *brown sugar* and boil over low heat for 2 minutes, stirring constantly. Stir in 2 tablespoons *milk* and bring just to a boil, stirring. Cool. Add 1 cup *powdered sugar*. Beat until thick enough to spread. Add a few drops hot water if it's too stiff. Spread over cake.

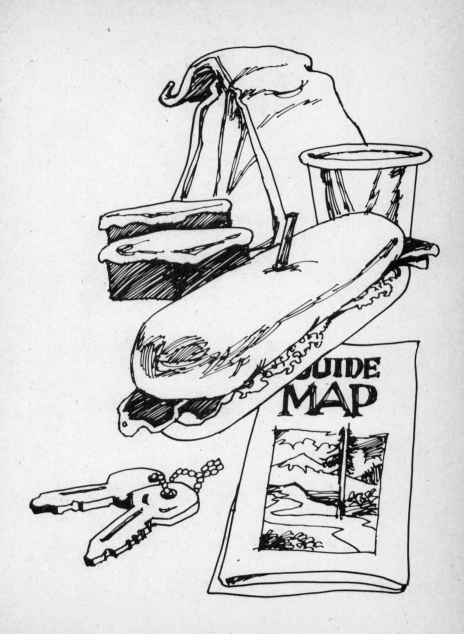

17
FOODS THAT TRAVEL

Black Ice

I knew going over the mountains was the bad
  part—Fog, snow, danger of ice.
I prayed a lot.
"Thank you, Lord, that You're there."
  "What do you mean 'there?'
  I'm *here*."

Applesauce Cake

Pour a can of *applesauce* into a colander and let
drain while you cream 1 cube *margarine*, 2 cups
sugar, and 2 *eggs*. When applesauce has quit drip-
ping you should have 1½ cups thick applesauce.
Blend into creamed mixture. Stir in 2½ cups
flour, ½ teaspoon *salt*, 2 teaspoons *soda*, ½ teaspoon *cinnamon*, ½ teaspoon *cloves*, ½ teaspoon
nutmeg, 1 cup chopped *raisins*, ½ cup *walnut
pieces*, add ½ cup *boiling water*. Pour into a greased
9" x 13" pan and bake 1 hour at 350°.

Frost with *Penuche Icing* from Chapter 16.

To travel: When icing is set, cut cake in squares and wrap each square in waxed paper or put in individual baggies.

Savory Strips

Combine ⅔ cup coarsely chopped *raisins*, ½ cup finely chopped cooked *ham* and ½ cup grated *cheddar cheese*. Stir in 2 cups *biscuit mix*, 1 teaspoon *dry mustard*, and ⅔ cup *milk*. Pat out the floured board to 10" x 6" rectangle and cut in 3" x ¾" strips.

Melt 1 cube *margarine*. Pour ¼ cup in bottom of 9" x 13" pan. Put in Savory Strips; pour remaining margarine over top. Bake at 450° for 15 minutes.

These are best eaten warm, so wrap in foil to travel.

Bacon Dogs

Fry 1 pound *bacon very* crisp. Pour out most of fat from grill. Lay 6 *hot dog buns,* cut sides down, on grill and toast lightly. Fill each bun with 5 or 6 strips of crisp bacon. Wrap in foil.

Jell-O Cups

If you have a cooler, fill small *paper cups* with your children's favorite flavor of *Jell-O*. Add *fruit, nuts,* or *marshmallows* as desired, but mine prefer it plain. Take along a package of *plastic spoons*.

Also . . .

Any of the cookies from Chapter 7 travel superbly. My daddy's travel favorite has always been simply mixing equal parts of *salted peanuts* and *raisins.* Of course, you'll need to take a BIG thermos of ice water and paper cups. Fresh fruit—especially apples—is really unbeatable travel food.

Damp wash clothes in plastic bags work better than any commercial wipe-ups they've invented yet.

Activities

After years of traveling with kids I should have tons of nifty activity advice—but it's probably because of all my experience that I know there's really not an awful lot that works all that well. Dot-to-dot books and Legos remain the perennial favorites in our family along with Twenty Questions, and the alphabet game—seeing who can get through the alphabet first, in order, from signs along the road. Keep a hymnal in the glove compartment for sing-alongs. Have you seen the crayons that are flat on one side so they won't roll around in the car?

My favorite as a child was the strip maps AAA used to make (maybe still do). You can make your own by marking your route on a fold-out roadmap with marking pen, X's for stopping spots, and cut into 3″ x 5″ strips. Assemble strips in order, with home on top, and staple together at the top of strips. These are easier for children to handle and to read than a fold-out map.

18

THE VERITABLE VEGETABLE

Vegetation Variation

"Sure, Pastor we'd love to keep the guest speaker from India this weekend . . . You say he's a VEGETARIAN?!"

Click.

Vegetables for a *whole* weekend—with *my* family?

Carrot-Cheese Ring with Peas

Cook and mash 2 pounds *carrots*—you should have 2 cups. Combine with 1 cup *cracker crumbs*, 1 cup *milk*, ¾ cup grated *sharp cheddar cheese*, 1 ⅓ cubes *margarine*, ¼ cup grated *onion*, 1 teaspoon *salt*, ¼ teaspoon *pepper*, dash *cayenne*.

Beat 2 *eggs* until puffy. Fold into carrot mixture. Pour into a well-greased 1½-quart ring mold. Bake at 350° for 45 minutes. Knife inserted in center should come out clean.

Turn onto warm platter. Fill center with 2 10-oz. packages frozen *peas*, cooked.

Cashew Rice

Brown 1 cup *brown rice* and 1 chopped *onion* in ¾ cube of *butter or margarine*. Add 3 teaspoons *chicken bouillon* and 3 cups *water*. Bring to a boil and simmer, covered, 45 minutes. Stir in 1 can *salted cashew nuts* and ½ cup *shredded coconut*. Heat through.

Cheese-Biscuit Ring

Melt ⅓ cup *margarine*. Brush angel food cake pan with 1 tablespoon of melted margarine. Cut ¼ pound colby or jack *cheese* into ½-inch cubes. Open 3 packages *whole wheat refrigerator biscuit dough*. Put a cube of cheese in the center of each biscuit and pinch dough up around it. Dip in melted margarine. Fill pan with 3 layers of cheese biscuits. Bake 25 minutes at 350°. Scatter remaining cheese cubes over top and bake 5 minutes longer or until browned.

Cool 5 minutes. Invert on serving platter. Brush with remaining margarine.

Whole Wheat Zucchini Cake

Peel and grate 2 cups *zucchini*. Mix with 1 cup melted *margarine*, 3 *eggs*, 1¼ cups *honey*, 3 cups *whole wheat flour*, ¾ teaspoon *baking powder*, 1 teaspoon *soda*, 1 teaspoon *salt*, 3 teaspoons *cinnamon*, ½ cup *unprocessed bran*. Bake in 2 loaf pans 50-60 minutes at 350° until toothpick inserted in center comes out clean.

For variety add ½ cup chopped *nuts* or *raisins*. Remember to simmer the raisins for 15 minutes first.

As bread, serve with *Honey Butter* (Chapter 6); as cake, serve with *cream cheese spread:* Whip together 1 cube *butter or margarine*, 3 ounces *cream cheese*, 1 teaspoon *vanilla*, and 2 cups *powdered sugar*.

And the next day for brunch:

Your Very Own Granola

The formula is to heat together ½ cup *vegetable oil*, 1 cup *honey*, 1 tablespoon *vanilla*, until honey melts. Pour over *12 cups dry ingredients*. Spread in thin layers on baking sheets and toast at 225° for 1½ hours, stirring once or twice.

Suggestions for dry ingredients are: *Wheat germ, sesame seeds, sunflower seeds, nuts, shredded coconut, rolled wheat, rolled oats, rye flakes, triticale, raisins, chopped dates, banana chips.* I've tried some rather wild things that happened to be on my shelf and so far I've found nothing that won't work.

Serve with a medley of *fresh, sliced fruits*, unflavored *yogurt*, and *honey. Or just milk* for the more traditional tastes.

Fat Veggie Omelette

Prepare filling first: In large skillet or fry pan combine 1 (16-oz.) can *whole potatoes*, drained and sliced, ½ pound *bacon**, chopped, 1 cup sliced *fresh mushrooms*, and 1 chopped *onion*. Sauté until bacon is crisp and onions are tender. Add 1 pound *fresh spinach*, washed and dried, to skillet and cover 5 minutes until wilted.

For omelette: Whip 4 *eggs whites* with ¼ cup *water* until soft peaks form. Beat 4 *egg yolks* with ¼ teaspoon *salt* and a dash of *pepper* until thick and creamy. Fold yolks and 1½ tablespoons *flour* into egg whites.

Melt 2 tablespoons *margarine* in 10-inch skillet over low heat. Pour in egg mixture and fry 3 minutes. Place pan in 325° oven for 12 minutes.

Meanwhile, make sauce: Blend ½ cup *mayonnaise*, 2 tablespoons *flour*, ¼ teaspoon *salt*, a dash of *pepper*, and ½ teaspoon *dry mustard* in small saucepan. Gradually add 1 cup *milk*. Cook and stir until thickened. Add 1 cup *shredded sharp cheddar cheese*, and 2 teaspoons *caraway seeds*. Heat until cheese melts.

To serve: Place omelette on large platter. Spoon filling on half of omelette; fold over. Pour sauce over top and serve it forth.

*If you're really making this for a vegetarian, leave out bacon and add 3 tablespoons *margarine*.

Finally, take him out to eat—he can order a grilled cheese on whole wheat and the kids can get HAMBURGERS!

19
CHRISTENING DAY MENU

Grandmother Rocks Elizabeth

"You have brought to our lives the truth of the Scripture: 'Children are an heritage of the Lord; and Children's children are the crown of old age.'

"You, little one, are 'blessed of the Lord which made heaven and earth.' I shall teach you of Him, just like Timothy's Grandmother Lois. So that it will be true in our family that 'All thy children shall be taught of the Lord; and great shall be the peace of thy children.'

"The Lord bless thee, and keep thee.
The Lord make His face to shine upon thee, and
  be gracious unto thee.
The Lord lift up His countenance upon thee, and
give thee peace.' "

Cranberry Ice
Put 4 cups *fresh cranberries* in a large pan with 2 cups *sugar* and 3½ cups *water*. Boil until berries

pop. Sieve. Add ½ cup *orange juice* and 2 table-spoons *lemon juice* to cranberry mixture. Pour in plastic containers and freeze.

To serve scoop into balls with ice cream scoop and place in well-chilled sherbert glasses. Serve as appetizer.

Cherry Fresh Ham

Tell your butcher you want a *whole fresh ham* with no water in it. Score the top in diamond patterns and place a *whole clove* in each diamond. Roast to an internal temperature of 160° on meat thermometer—about 15 minutes per pound in a 325° oven. This will take 3 hours and 45 minutes for a 15 pound ham, or if you want to roast it slower, about 5 hours in a 250° oven.

Combine ½ cup *brown sugar* and ½ cup *honey.* During the last hour of baking baste with honey mixture every 15 minutes.

Cherry sauce: Combine 1½ tablespoons *cornstarch*, ¼ cup *sugar*, ¼ teaspoon *allspice*, ¼ teaspoon *ground cloves* in saucepan. Drain 1 can *sour red pitted cherries* and add juice to ingredients in pan. Cook and stir over medium heat until thick and clear. Add cherries and a few drops *red food coloring.*

Serve over hot baked ham slices.

French Beans

Sauté ¼ cup chopped *onion* and ¼ cup *slivered almonds* in 2 tablespoons *butter* until almonds are toasted.

Steam (or boil if you don't have a vegetable steamer) 2 packages frozen *French sliced green beans.* Top with onions and almonds. If it's near

Christmastime, add a few strips of *pimiento*, too.

Escalloped Pototoes

Quarter and cook 8 medium *potatoes* with their skins on. Cool, peel, and cube finely.

Melt ¼ cup *butter*. Add ⅓ cup finely chopped *onions* and sauté for 2 minutes. Add 1 can *cream of chicken soup*, 2 cups *sour cream*, and 1½ cups grated *sharp cheddar cheese*. Mix in potatoes gently. Place in a large baking pan and bake 45 minutes at 350°.

Scandinavian Crescents

In a large bowl combine: 4 cups *flour*, 1 teaspoon *salt*, ¼ cup *sugar*. Cut in 1 cup *butter or margarine*. Add 1 package *dry yeast*, dissolved in ¼ cup *warm water*, 3 *egg yolks*, and 1 cup *lukewarm milk*.

Mix well, cover, and refrigerate overnight. (It will not rise.) Roll half the dough into an 18″ x 6″ rectangle. Cut in triangles, 2″ long at wide end. Brush with a little melted butter. Starting at wide end, roll up and place on baking sheet, curving each to a crescent shape. Cover and let rise in a warm place 1 hour, until a dent remains when dough is pressed with a finger. Bake at 375° for 15 to 20 minutes until lightly browned.

Serve with butter and jam.

Frozen Strawberry Mousse

Mix together 1½ cups *flour*, ½ cup *brown sugar*, ¾ cup *walnut bits*, and ¾ cup melted *butter*. Spread on a cookie sheet and bake at 350° for 20 minutes. Cool and break up into crumblies. Set aside ⅓ of mixture. Spread remainder over bottom of 9″ x 13″ pan.

Combine in large mixing bowl: 2 *egg whites*, 2 tablespoons *lemon juice*, ¾ cup *sugar*, 1 large box *frozen strawberries* and 1 small box *frozen strawberries*. Beat with electric mixer on high speed. Fold in a 14½-ounce carton *frozen whipped topping*. Pour over layer in pan, sprinkle on reserved crunchies, freeze. Cut in squares to serve.

If desired, spoon a few *frozen strawberries*, with juice, over top of each serving.

This menu is for a baby girl—I can't remember what we had for the boys—probably pizza or hamburgers, if their current eating habits are any indication.

20

REHEAT AT 350° FOR 20 MINUTES

Ladies Retreat

"What are you retreating from? Seems to me you should be advancing."

"Very funny."

"But Mom, you'll come back and fix our meals, won't you?"

Meal #1
Cowboy Casserole

Fry one pound *hamburger* with 1 large chopped *onion* and ½ minced *green pepper*. Drain. Add: ½ teaspoon *garlic powder*, 1 teaspoon *chili powder*, 1 No. 2 can *tomatoes*, cut, with liquid; ½ cup uncooked *rice;* 1 No. 2 can *kidney beans*, drained.

Pour into 2-quart casserole and bake covered 1 hour at 350°.

Overnight Salad
(No-no! Don't reheat the salad!)

Put in a large salad bowl, one layer at a time: ½

head shredded *lettuce*, ½ cup chopped *celery*, ½ *green or red pepper* chopped, 1 can *sliced water chestnuts* drained, 1 package (10-oz.) *frozen green peas* still frozen. Top with enough *mayonnaise* to cover (about 1 cup), 1 cup grated *cheddar cheese*, 4 strips *bacon*, fried crisp and crumbled.

Cover and refrigerate overnight. You can toss this before serving, or leave it in layers.

Casserole Bread

In a large bowl combine 1½ cups *flour*, 1 cup *whole bran cereal*, 1 package *dry yeast*.

In saucepan heat 1 cup *water*, 1 cup *applesauce*, ¼ cup *margarine*, 2 tablespoons *brown sugar*, and 1 teaspoon *salt* until margarine melts (120°). Add to flour mixture and beat 3 minutes with electric mixer. Stir in 1½-2 cups more *flour* by hand to make a soft dough. Beat well.

Cover and let rise in warm place until double, about 1 hour. Punch down and turn into greased 2-quart casserole. Let rise again until double, about 40 minutes.

Bake at 350° for 1 hour. Rub with a stick of *margarine* while hot—about 1 tablespoon should melt in. Serve from casserole, with *Honey Butter*, if desired.

Chocolate Pudding Cake

Combine 1 cup *flour*, 1 teaspoon *baking powder*, ¼ teaspoon *salt*, ¾ cup *sugar*, 1½ teaspoon *cocoa*. Stir in ½ cup *milk*, 2 tablespoons melted *margarine*, 1 teaspoon *vanilla*, ½ cup chopped *nuts* if desired. Spread in well-greased 8" x 8" pan.

Sprinkle 1 cup *brown sugar* and 3 tablespoons

cocoa over batter. Pour 1¾ cups *hot water* over all. Bake 45 minutes at 350°.

Serve warm with thick *cream.*

Meal #2

Drive 2 miles east, turn left, drive 3 blocks, look for the golden arches.

21
FOOD FOR KIDS

A Mother's Instructions

Raise up a child in the way he should go . . .

"Dear God, they are all so beautiful.
Please keep them safe—no accidents, no
   diseases.
Such awful things can happen.
They all have such fine minds,
Help them develop them in lines you choose.
Don't let them get lost in intellectual tangents,
Don't let them fail to develop the talents you've
   given them.

"And now, God, they've all known You from
   their earliest memories.
Don't let them be led astray by worldly
   philosophies or desires.
Don't let the tempter . . ."
"The Father gave me twelve and I kept all of
   them, save the son of perdition.

You have given me four.
I can keep them too."

Spider Cookies

You will need: 1 package *rope licorice,* cut in 3"
pieces, 1 can *vanilla icing,* 1 package *chocolate
wafer cookies,* a few *chocolate chips.*

Spread icing on 1 chocolate wafer, lay 4
licorice strips across for legs, spread another
wafer with icing and place on top of legs. Put 2
dabs of white icing on top at front and place
chocolate chips on for eyes.

You can plan a whole Halloween party around
this theme: Give spider rings (from dime store)
for favors, and read the children's book *Be Nice
To Spiders* (from public library) using a black
glove, with white eyes on top, for a puppet. Pin
legs on a spider, rather than tails on a donkey,
and play musical pillows, rather than musical
chairs, letting children crawl around like spiders,
instead of marching to music.

Snoopy Salad

You will need: *Canned pear halves, prunes,
raisins, canned bing cherries,* and *mandarin
oranges.* Drain canned fruit.

Arrange pear half cut side down on plate, use
cherry for nose, raisin for eye, prune for ear, and
2 orange sections for bow at top of neck.

Should probably be served with PEANUTS
butter sandwiches—which could start the theme
for another party.

Ice Cream Cone Cakes

You will need: 1 package *chocolate, strawberry,*

or *vanilla cake mix;* 24 flat bottomed *ice cream cones; icing mix* in chocolate, strawberry *or* vanilla; *chocolate sprinkles, fresh strawberries* or *marachino cherries, or sugar cookie sprinkles.*

Prepare cake mix according to package directions, adding 2 tablespoons *margarine* to ingredients. Divide batter into ice cream cones, stand up in muffin tins and bake 15 minutes, until done. Cool. Prepare your choice of icing and frost "ice cream cones," decorating chocolate with chocolate sprinkles, strawberry with fresh strawberry or cherry, vanilla with sprinkles.

If you want to serve ice cream, too, just for fun cut it in squares and serve with forks, like cake.

"Caramel Apple" Popcorn Balls

Melt ½ pound *marshmallows* with 1 stick *margarine.* Stir in 1 popper (about 4 quarts) *popcorn.* Oil hands and shape into balls. Cover each ball with *"Wrapple"* (sheet of caramel prepared for wrapping apples) and insert popsicle *stick.*

Frozen Bananas

Peel 8 *bananas,* place on cookie sheet and pop in freezer until hard.

Melt a package of *artificially flavored chocolate chips* in top of double boiler. Dip bananas in chocolate, then in *butter brickle bits* (they come in packages like chocolate chips), or in *nuts.*

Remember these recipes when it's your turn for kindergarten snack day or to be room mother for a party.

22

FOOD FOR TEENS

Teen Talent Take-Off

"Good luck in the contest, dear. I know your choir will do well."

"Mumble, mumble, mumble." Door slam. "Bye."

"Wait! You told them what?"

"Mumble, mumble, mumble, gotta go."

"Stan! I'm afraid to ask, but did *your* son just say he was bringing the whole choir back here afterwards?"

"Yes, that's what it sounded like."

"I think I'd rather not know, but did he also say he told them just to bring money and I'd fix the food because I just *love* to cook?"

Bologna/Cheese Dogs

Dice ½ pound *garlic bologna* and ½ pound *sharp cheddar cheese* cut into ¼-inch cubes. Toss with ⅓ cup sliced *green onions* and ½ cup sliced *pimiento olives.* Stir in 3 tablespoons *mayonnaise* and ½ cup *chili sauce.* Mix well and spread on 12 *hot dog buns.* Wrap in foil and bake 15 minutes at 350°.

Better plan to provide 2 for each boy. The girls will want seconds, but will be embarrased to eat that much.

Cold Dip for Veggies

Stir together 1 envelope *ranch dressing mix* with 1 cup *sour cream* and 1 cup *mayonnaise.* Wash and cut into finger food size: Small head *cauliflower,* 1 bunch *broccoli* stalks, 1 bunch *radishes, cherry tomatoes,* fresh *mushrooms,* 2 *cucumbers,* 2 *parsnips,* and of course, *carrots* and *celery.*

Hot Dip for Chips

Brown 1 pound *hamburger* and 1 bunch *green onions,* chopped. Drain. Add a 4-oz. can chopped *chili peppers,* 1 teaspoon *Worcestershire sauce,* a 4-oz. can *tomato sauce* and 1 pound grated *cheddar cheese.* Serve from electric skillet to keep warm.

The kids will go through 2 or 3 kinds of chips, but *tortilla chips* are best with this.

Shrimp Salad

Cook 1 cup *macaroni.* Drain and chill. Mix with 1 can *deveined shrimp,* drained, 2 stalks chopped *celery,* 4 *hard-boiled eggs,* chopped, 2 handfuls of shredded *luttuce* and enough *mayonnaise* to moisten, about 1 cup. Diced *sweet pickle* may be added, if desired.

Lemon Fizz

These recipes are spicy—you'll need a lot to drink. Prepare *frozen lemonade* according to directions on can, substituting *7-Up* for water. When its all gone, give them ice water.

No discussion of food for teens would be complete without pizza. Here are my 2 favorites:

Individual Pizzas

Brown 1 pound *hamburger* and ¼ cup chopped *onion*. Drain off fat. Add 1 teaspoon *Worcestershire sauce*, ¾ teaspoon *salt*, ¼ teaspoon *pepper*, 1 (8-oz.) can *tomato sauce*, ¼ teaspoon *oregano*. Cover and simmer a few minutes.

Place 10 *English muffin* halves on a baking sheet. Top with meat sauce. Cut 4 large Mozzarella slices in thirds and place on pizzas. Broil just long enough to melt cheese.

Whooeee, It's Time for Pizzee!

Prepare ½ box *hot roll mix* according to package directions for pizza crust. Pre-bake for 10 minutes at 450°.

To prepare sauce combine ¼ cup chopped *onion*, 6 ounces *tomato paste*, ½ teaspoon *salt*, ¼ teaspoon *pepper*, ¼ teaspoon *oregano*, 1/8 teaspoon *garlic powder*, and a dash of *cayenne pepper*. Spread over pizza crust.

Grate half of an 8-oz. *Mozzarella cheese* and sprinkle it over sauce. Fry and drain ½ pound *hamburger*, put over cheese. Grate a large stick of *pepperoni* over hamburger. Place in oven at 450° for 10 minutes.

Slice rest of the *cheese*. Remove pizza from oven, place cheese slices on it, and return to oven just long enough to melt cheese. It's ready!

for Baby

23

SHOWERS OF BLESSING

I Know I Volunteered . . .

"What shall we serve for Maureen's shower Thursday?"

"Thursday?!"

"Sure, it has been on the calendar for ages. You volunteered to be chairman, remember."

"Yes, I know I volunteered. I just didn't know it was the same night as PTA open house and Stan's Sunday school board meeting."

Spring Showers

Frozen Lemon Mousse: Combine 1½ cups *graham cracker crumbs*, ¼ cup melted *butter*, and 2 tablespoons *powdered sugar*. Press in bottom of 9" x 13" pan. Bake just 5 minutes at 325°. Cool.

Beat 6 *egg yolks* and juice and grated rind of 2 *lemons* until frothy. Gradually beat in 1 cup *sugar*. Continue beating at least 5 minutes until thick and lemon-colored.

Beat 6 *egg whites* with ¼ teaspoon *cream of tartar* until stiff. Fold egg whites and 1 cup *sour cream,* whipped, into egg yolk mixture.

Pour over crumb crust and freeze. Serves 12.

Note: Spring Showers and Winter Showers recipes are both frozen. Have serving trays chilled and set portions out only as guests arrive. The lemon is especially delicate.

Summer Showers

Individual Strawberry Trifles: Prepare 1 package yellow *cake mix* according to package directions, adding 2 tablespoons *margarine* and 1 teaspoon *vanilla* to ingredients. Bake in 9" x 13" pan. Cool and cut into cubes. Divide cubes among 24 1-cup clear plastic disposable tumblers.

Thaw 2 packages (16 ounces each) *frozen strawberries* and spoon over cake pieces with juice. Prepare 2 packages (4¾ oz.) *vanilla pudding mix* (not instant) according to package directions and spoon over berries. Chill several hours.

Whip 2 cups *heavy cream* with ¼ cup *sugar* and 2 teaspoons *vanilla.* Top trifles with whipped cream. Garnish with fresh *strawberries* or toasted, slivered *almonds.* Serves 24.

Fall Showers

Let's do something different and serve trays of sweet breads, cheese, and fruit.

Lemon Poppy Bread: Beat together 1 package *lemon cake mix* (not with pudding in mix), ½ cup *cooking oil,* 1 small package *coconut cream pudding mix,* 4 *eggs,* 2 tablespoons *poppy seeds,* ½ teaspoon *lemon extract,* and 1 cup *water.*

Bake in 2 loaf pans at 350° for 40 minutes. Spread slices with *butter.*

Carrot Nut Bread: Beat 2 cups *sugar* and 4 *eggs* until thick. Stir in 1⅓ cups *oil,* 1 teaspoon *soda,* 2 cups *flour,* 2 teaspoons *baking powder,* 2 teaspoons *cinnamon,* 4 cups grated *carrots,* and ¾ cup *walnut pieces.* Turn into greased and floured angel food cake pan and bake at 350° for 1 hour.

Serve with *Cream Cheese Spread:* Mix 8 ounces *cream cheese,* ½ cup *butter,* 1 teaspoon *vanilla,* 1 box *powdered sugar.* Beat well.

Ladies doing serving should cut a few slices of *fruit* at a time from a large fruit bowl, or cut pieces ahead and stir in 2 tablespoons of *ascorbic acid fruit freshener.* Offer fruit pieces on toothpicks.

See chapter 3 for suggestions on *cheese selection.* Don't cut cheeses ahead or they will dry out. Have a cutting knife for each variety and invite guests to serve themselves.

Winter Showers

Chocolate-Mint Delight: Crush 28 *vanilla wafers* and toss with ¼ cup melted *butter.* Reserve ¼ cup and press remaining crumbs into bottom of 9″ x 9″ pan. Bake at 325° for only 5 minutes. Cool.

Spread with 1 quart *peppermint stick ice cream,* softened. If you can't get peppermint stick ice cream, crush 1 cup *peppermints* (in a plastic bag with a hammer) and stir into 1 quart *vanilla ice cream.* Freeze.

Melt ½ cup *butter* and 2 squares *unsweetened*

chocolate over low heat. Stir in 3 well-beaten *egg yolks*, 1½ cups *powdered sugar*, ½ cup *pecan pieces*, and 1 teaspoon *vanilla*. Beat 3 *egg whites* stiff and fold in chocolate mixture. Spread over ice cream. Top with reserved crumbs. Serves 8 generously.

For an inexpensive and unusual punch, try a fruit flavored *sun tea*. Buy a box of *fruit-flavored herbal tea* from a tea specialty shop—my favorite is Really Raspberry. Put 2 bags in a glass gallon jar of *cool water*, cover, and let sit in the sun for an hour. Serve with lots of ice—ice tea without ice is unthinkable.

Activities

Thinking up games for showers is almost as painful as having to play them. Thank goodness most showers are drop-in these days. But if you want to offer a few different activities you might: Have a formal guest book for guests to register with their complete address—saves hours when writing thank you notes. Have a file box and cards decorated with stick-on roses: guests fill out cards giving bits of advice to new bride or new mother—hints for entertaining small children on rainy days, how to keep "Zing" in your marriage, etc. My 80-year-old grandmother wrote, "Always fix him a nice hot breakfast." Eighteen years later I'm still at it; Have a pile of magazines, scissors, glue, marking pens at a table. Guests compile a scrapbook of guest-of-honor's life—past, present, and future.

24

SUNDAY SCHOOL CLASS PARTY

Brainstorming

"They want something easy, inexpensive, fun, and different. Any ideas? . . . Well, don't all talk at once."

"Potatoes are inexpensive."

"And easy. Especially baked."

"But fun and different?"

"Sure. We'll make a whole meal out of them with fancy toppings. Each member of the committee can make a different kind of sauce. It'll be great—I can't wait!"

"And now about the program . . . Well, don't all talk at once."

"Table games?"

"We did that last time."

"Music?"

"We did that time before last."

"How about a soiré?"

"For a Sunday school party? It sounds decadent!"

"I know. That's what hooks people. Actually it's a French word for intellectual salon."

"Eeek! That sounds dull!"

"That's why you call it a soiré."

The Plan

Contact 5 or 6 people from your class ahead of time and ask them to come prepared with a 5-10 minute presentation—anything they want to do. Ideas to get them started are: Book reviews (C.S. Lewis *The Great Divorce, The Frantic Mother Cook Book*, children's literature—anything goes), devotionals, poetry readings (especially original poetry), personal sharings of what God is doing in your life right now, paintings or craft projects, music.

Schedule for the evening: Salad bar, 4 presentations, potato meal, 2 presentations, Hymn of Praise (page 129), dessert, coffee and tea.

Salad Bar

See Chapter 5 for directions.

Bacon Dressing: Fry 3 slices *bacon* crisp. Remove and crumble. Sauté 2 tablespoons finely chopped *onion* in bacon fat for 2 or 3 minutes. Drain on paper towel. Combine bacon and onion, ½ cup *mayonnaise*, 2 tablespoons *corn syrup*, ¼ teaspoon *salt*, 1 teaspoon *honey*, 1 tablespoon *milk*. Chill.

Sour Cream Dressing: Combine 1 cup *sour cream*, 2 teaspoons *terragon vinegar*, 1 tablespoon *white vinegar*, 1 teaspoon *horseradish*, ½ teaspoon *salt*, and ¼ teaspoon *pepper*.

Warm Tomato Dressing: Combine 1 clove

minced and mashed *garlic*, 1 teaspoon *salt*, ¼ teaspoon *pepper*, ¼ teaspoon *dry mustard*, ½ teaspoon *paprika*, ½ teaspoon *sugar*, ¼ cup *red wine vinegar*, 1 can *stewed tomato pieces*, 1 cup *olive oil*. Heat, stirring to blend. Serve warm. If oil separates, stir occasionally.

Homemade Croutons: Cut 4 slices of *bread* in cubes, sauté in ¼ cup melted *butter* with 1 clove finely minced *garlic* until bread cubes are golden on all sides. Drain on paper towels. These are great—better double the recipe.

Potato Meal

Bake one large *potato* per person. Some of the ladies will only want half and some will want seconds, so you should come out just right. Scrub potatoes with a good stiff brush and oil skins. Place right on rack on a 350° oven for 1 hour. Do NOT wrap in foil—this makes them sticky inside. Inserting 3-inch aluminum nails in center of potatoes helps them cook more evenly.

Wearing mitts, cut a deep gash lengthwise in the potato and make a smaller cut crosswise. Squeeze and push from both ends to open potato. Let guests ladel on topping of their choice. Have bowls of freshly snipped *parsley* and grated *cheddar cheese* for topping the toppings.

Hamburger Chow Chow: Fry 1½ pounds *hamburger* and 1 chopped *onion* until hamburger is brown. Drain off oil. Stir in 1 cup chopped *celery*, 1 small can *mushroom pieces with liquid*, *1 can cream of mushroom soup*, 1 can *cream of chicken soup*, ½ soup can *water*, 1 teaspoon *salt*, ¼ teaspoon *pepper*, 1 teaspoon *Worcestershire sauce*. Bring just to a boil, cover and simmer 1 hour.

Cashew Chicken: Sauté ¼ cup chopped *onion* and ¼ cup chopped *celery* in 2 tablespoons *margarine*. Add 4 cups diced cooked *chicken*, 1 can *cream of chicken soup*, 1 can *chicken broth*, 1 tablespoon *soy sauce*. Bring to boiling, cover, and simmer half an hour. Stir in ⅔ cup *cashew nuts*.

Ranchero Chili: Sauté 1 finely chopped *green pepper* and ¼ cup finely chopped *onion* in 2 tablespoons *oil* until tender. Add 1 cup *chili sauce*, 1 can *tomato sauce with tomato pieces*, 2 tablespoons *lemon juice*, 1 teaspoon *Worcestershire sauce*, ¼ teaspoon *chili powder*, 1 can *chili without beans*. Bring to boiling, cover, and simmer 15 minutes.

Tuna à la King: Sauté one small chopped *cream of celery soup*, ½ can *milk*, 1 can *mushroom pieces* with liquid, 1 jar *chopped pimientos* with liquid, ½ bottle *stuffed olives*, sliced, 1 can *solid white tuna*, drained and flaked. Bring to a boil, cover and simmer 15 minutes.

Curried Eggs: Sauté 3 sliced *onions* in 1 cube *margarine*. Add ¼ teaspoon *salt* and ¼ cup *flour*. Blend well. Add 1 tablespoon *curry powder* and 2 cups *chicken broth*. Cook and stir until sauce comes to a boil and thickens. Gently stir in 1 dozen *hard-boiled eggs*, quartered, ¼ cup *white raisins* and ¼ cup toasted *slivered almonds*.

Cheesey Veggies: Blend ⅓ cup *mayonnaise* with 2 tablespoons *flour*, ¼ teaspoon *salt*, ½ teaspoon *dry mustard*, a dash of *pepper* in a small saucepan. Stir in 1 cup *milk*. Cook and stir until thickened. Add 1 cup grated *sharp cheddar cheese*, 1 jar chopped *pimiento*, and 1 10-ounce bag *mixed vegetables*, thawed. Simmer 15 minutes. If too thick add a bit more milk.

Oreo Mint Dessert

Crush 1 package *Oreo cookies* and toss with 6 tablespoons melted *margarine*. Set aside ¼ cup. Press remainder in an 8" x 8" pan.

Put 1 cup *butter mints* in plastic bag and crush with hammer. Fold mints, 1 cup *miniature marshmallows,* and a few drops *green food coloring* into 2 cups *heavy cream,* whipped. Pour over chocolate crust. Top with reserved crumbs. REFRIGERATE FOR 2 OR 3 DAYS. Serves 12.

Hymn of Praise

Borrow rhythm instruments from kindergarten department or a school teacher friend. Instruct group that we are going to prepare a performance of praise—with God as our audience. Distribute copies of script and assign parts. Rehearse 3 or 4 times before actual "performance."

Psalm 150

Solo voice: Praise ye the Lord.

Ladies: Praise God in his sanctuary,

Men: Praise Him in the firmament of his power

Ladies: Praise him with the psaltery and harp.
S   S
Solo female: Praise him with the timbrel
S
and dance;
(tambourine strike with S)

	G
Solo male:	Praise him with stringed in-

                              C
          struments and organs.
          (autoharp chords on marked
          words)

Men: Praise him upon the loud cym-
              bals. X
          (Cymbal crash on X)

          *   *   *   *   *   *
Women: Praise him upon the high-
              sounding cymbals. X
                      *   * *
          (triangle on *; Cymbal on X)
          =   =   =   =   =
All: Let everything that hath breath
              praise the Lord.
          (wood blocks on =)
          +   +   +   +
All: Praise ye the Lord. X
          (sticks on +; cymbals on X)

25
TAKE-OUT COVERED DISHES

Church Dinner

"Hello . . . Oh, hi, Shiela . . . The church dinner?. . .Ohhhh, I forgot it was tonight. What are we supposed to bring? . . . Casserole and vegetable. Gotcha . . . A family that eats like mine should bring 2 of each? Right. See you tonight."

Click.

Just a Good Dish

While 8 ounces of *macaroni* are cooking in boiling water, brown 1½ pounds *hamburger* and 4 chopped *onions*. Drain water from macaroni and fat from hamburger. Combine with 1 can *whole tomatoes*, cut up, 1 can *kidney beans*, drained, 1 teaspoon *salt*, and ¼ teaspoon *pepper*.

Spread in 9" x 13" pan and sprinkle with lots of grated *cheddar cheese*. Bake at 350° for 20 minutes until well heated.

Pam's Potatoes

Scrub 5 *potatoes* and cut into ½-inch cubes (yes, leave peelings on). Steam, or cook in small amount of boiling water, 15 minutes. Drain, if boiled.

Stir in 2 cups *cottage cheese*, 1 cup *sour cream*, 4 *green onions*, chopped—include stems about halfway up, ½ teaspoon *garlic salt*, ½ teaspoon *salt*, ¼ teaspoon *pepper*.

Bake in a 9" x 13" pan for 30 minutes at 350°. During last 10 minutes top with 1 cup grated *cheddar cheese*.

5-Layer Dinner

In a 2-quart casserole crumble ½ pound *hamburger* on bottom (uncooked), cover with a layer of 3 sliced *potatoes* (scrub and leave skins on), then 4 stalks *celery*, diced, 1 medium *onion*, diced. Pour 2 cups *canned tomatoes* over all. Bake at 350° for 1 hour.

Green Beans Delicious

Empty 2 cans *cut green beans* into a large saucepan and let them boil briskly while you prepare sauce. Sauté ¼ cup *sliced almonds* in 2 tablespoons *margarine* until lightly browned. Add 2 tablespoons finely chopped *onion*. When onion is tender blend in 1 can *mushroom soup*.

Drain beans (the liquid should be almost boiled away), place in flat casserole and pour sauce over top. Top with ½ cup grated *cheddar cheese*. Heat at 350° for 15 minutes.

Frankfurter Goulash

Combine 2 cups *macaroni*, cooked; 1 small can

spaghetti sauce with meat; ¼ pound jack *cheese,* cubed; 1 small can *sliced mushrooms,* drained; ½ cube *margarine,* melted; and 1 teaspoon *salt.* Bake in 9" x 13" pan for 20 minutes at 350°.

Cover top of pan with slices of *cheddar cheese* and 1 package *hot dogs.* Sprinkle hot dogs with *season salt.* Return to oven until hot dogs swell, about 10 minutes.

Scalloped Corn

Fry 3 slices *bacon* crisp. Sauté ¼ cup minced *onion* and ¼ cup minced *green pepper* in bacon fat. Add 1 can *cream style corn* and 1 cup *milk*—heat.

Fold 2 beaten *eggs,* ⅓ cup *cracker crumbs,* and 1 small jar *diced pimiento* into corn mixture. Turn into 1½-quart buttered casserole, top with crumbled bacon and bake 30 minutes at 350° until firm.

26
NOT-SO-CHANCY POTLUCK

Announcement

To our Visitors:

You have honored us with your presence in our worship service today. We hope you will also honor us with your presence at dinner immediately following the morning service in the fellowship hall. Your whole family is invited.

To our Members:

For the next 6 weeks this summer, each adult Sunday school class will be hosting a Sunday dinner welcome for its class members, their families, and our visitors. Each member family is asked to bring a molded salad and a pan cake. Main dish, rolls, and vegetable will be furnished (donations appreciated).

Orange Delight

Soften 2 envelopes *unflavored gelatin* in ½ cup *cold water*. Add 1 cup *boiling water* and stir until dissolved. Stir in 1½ cups *orange juice*, 1 table-spoon *lemon juice*, ⅔ cup *sugar*, 1 can drained *mandarin oranges*, 1 can drained *pineapple tidbits* (use *pineapple juice* in place of water), ½ cup chopped *nuts*. Pour into mold and chill until firm.

Ruby Beet Ring

Soften 1½ tablespoons *gelatin* in ¼ cup *cold water*. Pour in 1¾ cups *boiling water* and stir until dissolved. Stir in ⅔ cup *sugar*, ½ cup *lemon juice*, 1 tablespoon *vinegar*, 1½ tablespoons *horseradish*, ½ teaspoon *salt*. Chill until partially thickened. Stir in 1 cup diced *celery*, ¾ cup finely chopped *cabbage*, ¾ cup *shoestring beets*. Pour into mold and chill until firm. Plain *yogurt* makes a tasty dressing for this.

Red Hot Apple Salad

Dissolve 1 package *cherry Jell-O* and ¼ cup *red hot candies* in 1½ cups *boiling water*. Add 3 or 4 *ice cubes* and stir until partially set. Add 1 cup chopped *apple*, ½ cup chopped *celery*, ½ cup chopped *nuts*. Pour into mold and chill until firm.

Mystery Salad

Drain 1 can *crushed pineapple*. Bring *juice* to boiling and dissolve 1 package *lemon jello* in it. Beat 1 3-ounce package *cream cheese* and 1 jar *diced pimiento*, drained, into jello mixture. Stir in 1 cup diced *celery* and ½ cup chopped *nuts*. When partially set, fold in 1 cup *heavy cream*, whipped. Pour into mold and chill until firm.

Cola Salad

Drain 1 No. 2 can *bing cherries* and 1 small can *crushed pineapple*. Add *water* to make 1½ cups liquid. Bring to boiling and add 1 package *raspberry Jell-O* and 1 package *cherry Jell-O*. Stir to dissolve. Stir in 2 small chilled bottles *Coke*. Chill until partially set. Stir in cherries and pineapple. Pour into mold and chill until firm.

Ham Baked for a Bunch

To serve 50 people you will need 20 pounds of *canned ham*. Remove from cans, warm uncovered at 300° until heated through (about 15 minutes per pound).

Serve with Raisin Sauce: Mix 2¼ cups *sugar* and ⅓ cup *cornstarch*. Stir into 1⅓ quarts *boiling water*. Cook and stir until sauce is clear and thickened, about 6 minutes. Stir in 1 teaspoon *cinnamon*, ¼ teaspoon *nutmeg*, 2 cups *orange juice*, ⅔ cup *lemon juice*, and 1 pound *raisins*. Simmer 10 minutes until raisins are plump.

Chicken Fried for a Flock

For 50 people you will need 35 pounds of *chicken parts*. This will be approximately 12-14 fryers.

Mix 6 cups *flour*, ½ cup *salt*, 2 tablespoons *paprika*, 1½ teaspoons *pepper*. Put about 1 cup in a heavy paper sack or plastic bag. Add about 3 pieces of chicken at a time and shake to coat well.

Melt 3 pounds *shortening* in shallow roasting pans. Place chicken parts in hot fat. Place in 400° ovens, uncovered, for 1 hour, turning 2 or 3 times.

To make gravy: Stir 2 cups *flour* into *drippings* in pans (this is a total of 2 cups, not 2 cups for each pan), add 1 gallon *milk* and cook and stir until thickened. Season with 2½ tablespoons *salt* and 1 teaspoon *pepper*. Simmer slowly until serving time.

Serve over *rolls*. You will need to buy 2 or 3 rolls per person.

Savory Zucchini

Cook 1½ pounds sliced *onions* in 1 cup hot *salad oil* until clear and yellow looking. Add 12 pounds sliced *zucchini*, 5 pounds *tomatoes* (if fresh, dip in boiling water, peel, and dice; if canned, drain and chop), 2½ tablespoons *salt*, 4 teaspoons *pepper*, and 2 tablespoons *oregano*. Cover and simmer 15 to 20 minutes, until zucchini is crisp-tender.

Oatmeal Cake

Pour 1½ cups *boiling water* over 1 cup *quick oatmeal*. Let cool. Cream together ½ cup *margarine*, 1 cup *white sugar*, 1 cup *brown sugar*, 2 *eggs*, 1 teaspoon *salt* and 1 teaspoon *cinnamon*. Stir in *oatmeal*. Add 1½ cups *flour* and 1 teaspoon *soda*. Bake in 9" x 13" pan for 30 minutes at 350°.

For topping: Combine 6 tablespoons melted *butter*, ⅔ cup *brown sugar*, 2 cups *crunchy granola cereal*, ¼ cup *cream*. 1 teaspoon *vanilla*. Spread on cake and broil for 2 minutes.

Chocolate Lovers' Cake

Dissolve 1 cup *cocoa* and ¾ cup *butter* in 2 cups *boiling water*. Cool. Stir in 2 cups *sugar*, 2 *eggs*, 2 cups *flour*, 1/8 teaspoon *salt*, 2 teaspoons *soda*, 4 teaspoons *vanilla*, and 2 tablespoons *vinegar*. Pour into 9" x 13" pan and bake for 35 minutes at 350°, until toothpick inserted in center comes out clean.

Top with icing from *When's Dessert Ready Cake* (Chapter 1), *Brownie icing* (Chapter 1), or *Gem Cake icing*, below.

Gem Cake

Cream 1 cup *butter*, 2 cups *sugar*, and 6 *eggs*. Add 3 cups *flour*, and 2 teaspoons *soda* alternately with 6 tablespoons *buttermilk* and 2 teaspoons *vanilla*. Pour into 9" x 13" pan. Drop 1 cup *blackberry jam* by spoonfuls onto the batter. Bake at 350° for 45 minutes until toothpick inserted in center comes out clean.

Sour Cream Frosting: Combine 1 box *powdered sugar*, 1 cube *butter or margarine*, ½ cup *sour cream*, 1 teaspoon *vanilla*. Beat until fluffy. Stir in ½ cup chopped *walnuts*, if desired.

All three of the above cakes are very moist and rich—that's the only way I like them.

Activities

When people come into the room put name tags on them—green for members, yellow for visitors. Also give each person ½ of a pair of words: Ball and Bat, Bread and Butter, Venice and Italy, Up and Down, etc. Tell them they are to find their partner and learn each other's name and 2 interesting facts about one another.

When everyone has been served, the emcee directs introductions by having each person stand up and introduce their partner: "I'm right and Dottie Jones is wrong. (Dottie stands.) She used to be a school teacher, but most recently she got down on the floor to teach her dog to bark."

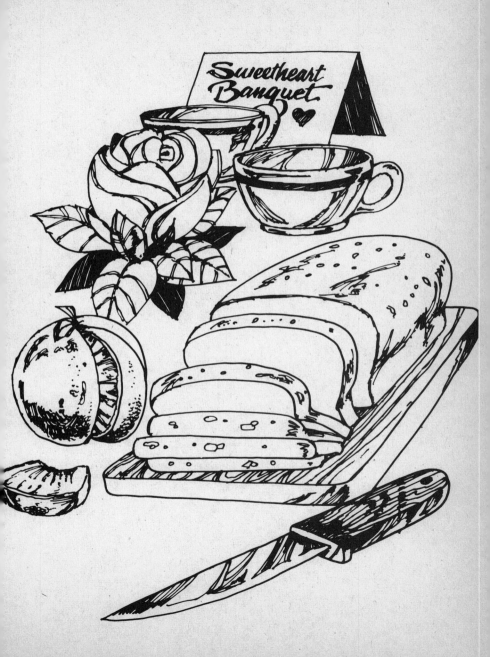

27

FOOD FOR FIFTY—
NIFTY AND THRIFTY

Let Me Call You Sweetheart

"Listen, I've got the *neatest* ideas for the Sweetheart Banquet this year! We'll have this giant red heart outline and each couple can pose framed in it for a photograph. Art got a new Polaroid so I'm sure he'll take the pictures for us.

"And then for the program Alan and Rebecca will sing 'The Hawaiian Wedding Song' and 'I Love you Truly' and Pastor can lead us all in renewing our wedding vows. It'll be soooo romantic!

"And I have this new red chiffon dress . . .

"Food? . . . I know potlucks are dull, but who could cook for fifty couples? It'd be too expensive if we had it catered."

Experts in the field of quantity cookery seem to agree that it's best not to attempt recipes that serve more than fifty—beyond that, amounts are hard to handle and quality is difficult to control.

So if your party is for fifty couples, prepare each recipe twice, rather than doubling it.

Punch Bowl

When guests arrive—over a little foot bridge, through an old-fashioned arbor, and into a garden setting with potted plants and wrought-iron furniture, have them greeted by your pastor's wife or hostess of honor presiding at a punch bowl.

Mix together in LARGE container (our church uses clean garbage cans, kept for that purpose) 3 quarts *ice water*, 1 quart frozen *orange juice concentrate*, 6 ounces *lemon juice*, 2 (#5) cans *pineapple juice*, 2 cups *sugar*, dissolved in 2 cups *water*, 1 quart *frozen strawberries*, undrained.

Put half of this base in punch bowl and add 2 quarts *ginger ale or 7-Up*. (Add 2 more quarts fizzy to remainder of base when it is used.)

This recipe will serve 100. To make sweetheart ice float, arrange 6 red rose buds, face down, in a heart-shaped cake pan of *distilled* water. Freeze. Unmold in punch bowl.

Ask the church youth group to serve as waiters and waitresses, wearing Sunday clothes and big smiles. If you promise a nice donation to their activity fund (youth groups always need money) they're sure to be delighted. They'll also be rather amused by the opportunity to watch "the old folks" acting like love birds.

Chicken Loaf Supreme

Stew 4 (4 pounds each) *stewing hens*. Remove meat and dice. Pour 1 pound *rice* in 1¼ quarts *boiling water* with 2 teaspoons *salt.* Cover and simmer 20 minutes.

Combine rice, chicken, 8 cups *dry bread crumbs,* 4 quarts plus 1 cup *chicken broth,* 16 *eggs,* 8 cups diced *celery* (buy about 2 pounds), 1 tablespoon *salt,* and 1 teaspoon *pepper.* Turn into 2 12" x 20" x 2" greased baking pans.

Melt 1 cube *margarine* and toss with crumb mixture and bake 1½ hours at 325°. Knife inserted in center should come out clean.

To serve, cut into squares, place on plates, and top with Chicken Sauce: Dice 4 *onions* and sauté in 1 cube melted *margarine.* Add 4 cans *cream of chicken soup* and 2 soup cans *milk.* Cook and stir until smooth.

Lemon-Mint Peas

Cook 7½ pounds *frozen peas* and 3 pounds *pearl onions.* Combine peas, onions, and 4 jars *diced pimiento,* drained. Stir in 1 pound *butter,* ¼ cup *lemon juice,* 1 teaspoon *grated lemon rind,* and ¼ cup *mint flakes.* Keep over warm heat until butter melts, stirring occasionally.

Ambrosia Salad

You will need a combination of about 12 pounds of *fresh or canned fruit* to make dinner salads (½-⅓ cup) for 50 people. Bananas, oranges, seeded grapes, and apples make a good combination. It's easier and more economical to buy *pineapple chunks* canned. You will need 2 quarts (or 4 pounds).

For dressing: Beat 1 dozen *eggs* until thick and lemon-colored. Beat in 1 quart *pineapple juice* (drained from pineapple chunks), juice of 4 *lemons,* and 2 cups *sugar.* Cook over boiling water until thick. Cool.

Whip 2 quarts *heavy cream* and fold in cooled egg mixture. Mix with fruits and chill well.

To serve on *lettuce leaves,* wash, dry, and chill 3 or 4 heads leaf lettuce. Sprinkle each serving with *flaked coconut.* You will need to buy 2 large bags.

French Bread
For 50 people, buy (at least) 7 loaves *French bread.* Cut loaves in 1-inch slices, wrap in foil, and heat at 350° for 15 minutes. It's such a disappointment to reach for a slice of bread and find it cold.

Either brush slices with melted *butter* before heating or set butter dishes on tables. You will need 1½ pounds of butter.

To keep bread warm foil-wrapped loaves should be placed in cloth napkins on bread trays.

Cherry Cheesecakes
Combine 1 pound *powdered sugar,* 2 teaspoons *cinnamon,* 1½ quarts *graham cracker crumbs,* and 1 cup melted *margarine.* Place about 1 cup crumb mixture in each of 6 (8'') cake pans and press firmly to form crust. Place in 325° oven for just 5 minutes.

Let 9 (8-oz.) packages of *cream cheese* stand until at room temperature. Beat in 11 *eggs,* 2¼ cups *sugar,* and 2 tablespoons *vanilla.* Pour over crusts—about 3 cups in each pan. Bake 30 minutes at 350° until knife inserted in center comes out clean.

Combine 5 cups *sour cream,* ½ cup *sugar,* and

1½ teaspoons *vanilla*. Pour 1 cup topping over each cake and return to oven for 10 minutes.

To serve, cut each cake in 8 pieces (this recipe serves 48). Open 6 cans *cherry pie filling* and spoon filling over each piece.

And now that you're experienced in quantity cookery, you'll surely want to try this 1763 English recipe from a Cornish cookbook:

Ingredients for a Great Cake

5 lbs. butter brought to a cream	Peel of 2 oranges
5 lbs. flour	Pint of canary
3 lbs. white sugar	½ pint rosewater
7 lbs. currants	43 eggs (half ye whites)
2/6 worth perfume	1 lb. citron

No instructions were given.

28
TRY IT ITALIAN

The Hospitable Hostess

"You know, Donna, our Bible study group is studying hospitality and it has really got me worried."

"Worried?"

"Yes, the commandment to hospitality is just that—a commandment. You've read the Scriptures: 'Be devoted to one another in brotherly love . . . practicing hospitality,' 'A church leader must be . . . hospitable,' 'Be hospitable to one another without complaint.' But that's not easy. To be honest, it's downright impossible for me."

"Well, the key to hospitality lies with the hostess. A good hostess is a relaxed hostess."

"Oh, great! Not only am I supposed to be this superhostess, I'm supposed to *relax*?"

It's not impossible, nor even difficult—just remember the Frantic Mother's six simple principles:

1. Plan a menu *you* like. Your guests are coming to your home to enjoy your environment. Don't try to duplicate what they would have in their home or in their favorite restaurant.

2. Plan a menu *you* are comfortable preparing. Friends tell me Chinese cooking is easy and great for entertaining. It is for them. I'd be a nervous wreck if I were to attempt it, since I don't know a wok from a wookie.

3. Do everything possible ahead—way ahead. Market the day before. Set your table early in the day or the day before. Plan how you'll cook and serve each course and set *everything* out. Still nervous? Write it all down.

4. *If* absolutely necessary, clean a day or two before. Remember—your house will always need it worse after the company has gone. And believe it or not, no one will notice! Okay, vacuum the living room and maybe dust a bit—but no turning out closets!

5. Concentrate on your guests and what interests them, *not* on your production. Good conversation with nothing but tea (so long as it was made according to the rules in Chapter 8) will make for a more successful party than haute cuisine with strained talk.

6. Don't fuss and don't apologize—*no matter what!* Bite your tongue if necessary, but don't do it. Nothing will make your guests feel more uncomfortable.

And when the evening's over, the last guest gone, and you collapse on the sofa with your feet up, how do you tell if it was a successful party? Ask youself one question—Did the hostess enjoy it?

Here is one of my favorite company menus. It is: Do-ahead, easy, pretty, guaranteed non-frantic, and it looks like you've slaved—Keep 'em fooled!

Antipasto Platter

Combine ¼ cup *olive oil*, 1 tablespoon *lemon juice*, ½ teaspoon *salt*, ¼ teaspoon *pepper*, ¼ cup *finely chopped scallions* (like an onion), 2 tablespoons freshly chopped *parsley*, (or 1 tablespoon parsley flakes). You may substitute ½ cup bottled Italian salad dressing, but this recipe is much better.

Cover a large platter with *lettuce leaves*. Drain a can of *white beans* (Great northern or navy) and pile in center of platter. Break a can of *solid white tuna* into chunks and place on beans. Fill the rest of platter with: *Black olives*, diagonally cut *carrot* and *celery* pieces, chunks of *provolone cheese*, thin slices of *salami*, and *cherry tomatoes*. Pour dressing over all. Chill.

When guests come have Antipasto Platter on coffee table with small napkins, saucers, toothpicks, and small forks.

Serve with sparkling grape juice or *Mock Champagne:* Mix 1 quart *apple juice* and 2 large bottles *ginger ale*. Chill well.

Do-ahead tip: About an hour before guests come fill water goblets ¾ full. Now all you have to do is drop 2 or 3 ice cubes in each glass before they come to the table.

Spaghetti

Brown 1 pound *hamburger* with 1 chopped

onion, 1½ teaspoons *garlic powder*, 1 teaspoon *salt*, ¼ teaspoon *pepper*, a dash of *cayenne*, ½ teaspoon *chili powder*, ½ teaspoon *Tabasco sauce*, 1 teaspoon *oregano*. Add 1 can *stewed tomatoes*, 1 can *mushroom soup*, 1 can *tomato soup*, 1 can *mushroom pieces*, with liquid. Simmer 1 hour.

Serve over cooked *spaghetti* and pass a bowl of *parmesan cheese*.

Olive Bread

Mix together: 1 cube *butter or margarine*, ¾ cup *mayonnaise*, 1 teaspoon *garlic powder*, 1 small can *chopped ripe olives*, 6 chopped *scallions (like an onion)*. Cut a loaf of French bread into 1″ slices and spead thickly with olive mixture. Slice a bottle of *stuffed green olives* and sprinkle over bread. Just before serving, broil until bubbly.

Piselli

Sauté ¼ cup finely chopped *onions* in 2 tablespoons *butter*. Add 1 package (10-oz.) *frozen peas*, thawed, and cook in butter about 3 minutes until tender. Stir in ¼ cup julienne strips of *prosciutto***** and heat through.

*(Prosciutto is Italian ham; if unavailable, substitute boiled ham.)

For your salad course arrange a few thinly sliced *mushrooms* and *tomato* slices on chilled *romaine* leaves on individual salad plates. Sprinkle with a few drops *lemon juice* and *olive oil* and a shake of *salt* and *pepper*.

Go ahead—serve your salad after the main course, continental style. It clears the palate and provides a respite before dessert.

Cassatta

That's Italian for cake—a memorable dessert is important for a party. Or else continue in the continental style and serve only *fresh fruit* and *cheese*—super simple is memorable too, especially if the fruit has served as a tempting centerpiece throughout the meal. Inviting big eaters? Do both—fruit and cheese last.

Buy a *pound cake* and cut it horizontally into ½'' slices. Beat 1 pound *cottage cheese* until very smooth. Beat in 2 tablespoons *heavy cream,* ¼ cup *sugar,* 3 tablespoons *orange juice,* 3 tablespoons chopped *citron,* and 2 ounces coarsely chopped *semisweet chocolate.*

Place 1 slice of cake on a serving platter, spread with cheese mixture, continue layers, ending with cake. Chill 2 hours until firm.

Melt 12 ounces *semisweet chocolate* in ¾ cup strong *coffee* over low heat, stirring constantly. Remove from heat and beat in ½ pound chilled *butter,* a small piece at a time. Beat smooth and chill until of spreading consistency. Spread thickly over cake. Pipe swirls on with decorator tube, if you wish.

Chill at least 24 hours. It's a good idea to make this even *2 days ahead* and wrap with plastic or foil. Then it's done and you don't have to worry about it until time to serve it to your admiring guests.

Serve with steaming black coffee.

29
ANNIVERSARY AT HOME

Surprise!

"It's our *what*!?"

"Anniversary, dear. Remember. That's the day we got married."

"Ooooh. I thought it was next week. Er, uh, want to go out to dinner?"

"Never mind, I already made reservations at our favorite restaurant."

"McDonalds?"

1. Get rid of the kids (just temporarily, of course).
2. Wear your prettiest dress—or better yet, negligee.
3. Put lots of candles on the table—even if he was kidding about forgetting the day, he won't bring flowers.

Melon Balls Melba
Scoop melon balls from a *cantaloupe* and

honeydew melon with melon baller. Chill.

Turn a 10-oz. package of *frozen raspberries* into a saucepan and heat until berries are thawed and soft. Press through a sieve to remove seeds. Return to saucepan with ½ cup *currant jelly* and 2 teaspoons *cornstarch* mixed with 1 tablespoon *cold water*. Cook until clear and thickened, stirring frequently. Chill.

Fill sherbet glasses with melon balls and drizzle with melba sauce.

Stroganoff

Brown 1 pound *hamburger* with ½ onion *chopped*. Drain off fat and add ¼ teaspoon *garlic powder*, 1 can *mushroom pieces* with liquid, 1 can *mushroom soup*, 1 jar *chopped pimientos*, 1 teaspoon *salt*, ¼ teaspoon *pepper*, ½ teaspoon *Worcestershire sauce*. Simmer at least half an hour.

Serve over *homemade noodles* from the frozen food department.

Stuffed Lettuce

Core 1 head *iceberg lettuce* and make a small hollow. (Save scraps for another salad.)

Mix 1 8-oz. package *cream cheese*, 1 tablespoon *mayonnaise*, 1 teaspoon *grated onion*, ¼ cup *grated carrot*, ¼ cup *minced green pepper*, ¼ cup peeled, minced, drained *tomato*, a few drops *Tabasco*, and ¼ teaspoon *salt*. Fill hollow in lettuce with this mixture. Wrap lettuce in plastic and chill well.

Slice crosswise about ¾" thick. Only cut the slices you plan to serve. Keep remainder tightly wrapped.

Parmesan Bread

More practical than garlic bread on your anniversary. Slice a loaf of *French bread* in 1'' slices. *Butter* generously on both sides. Sprinkle ¼ cup *parmesan cheese* on a plate. Dip buttered slices in cheese and toast on grill or electric fry pan until golden.

Angel Pie

Beat 2 *egg whites* with a dash of *salt*, ¼ teaspoon *cream of tartar*, and ½ cup *sugar* until very stiff. Fold in ½ teaspoon *vanilla* and ½ cup finely chopped *nuts*. Pile in a lightly greased 8'' pie pan and shape to pan. Bake 275° for 50-60 minutes. You don't want to brown your meringue crust, just to dry it. Cool.

Melt 1 bar *sweet baking chocolate* in 3 tablespoons *water*. Stir in 1 teaspoon *vanilla* and 3 teaspoons *powdered sugar*. Beat 1 cup *whipping cream* and fold in cooled chocolate mixture. Pile in meringue crust. Refrigerate until serving time.

30

LUNCHEON FOR MY MOTHER

Check-Up

Though a mother speaks with the tongues of men and of angels, and has not Christian love, she is become as sounding brass, or a tinkling cymbal.

And though she has the gift of prophecy, and understands all mysteries, and all knowledge, and though she has all faith, so that she could remove mountains, and has not Christian love, her relationship to her family is only filial, and often little more than biological.

And though she bestows all her goods to feed the poor, and though she gives her body to be burned, and has not Christian love, it profits her nothing and everyone else very little.

But a mother's Christian love suffers long, and is kind. Her Christian love envieth not; her Christian love vaunteth not itself, is not puffed up, doth not behave itself unseemly, seeketh not her own benefit, is not easily provoked, does not consider doing evil.

Her Christian love rejoiceth not in iniquity, but rejoiceth in the truth. Her Christian love beareth all things, believeth all things, hopeth all things, endureth all things.

A mother's Christian love never fails, because it is not her own, but Christ's love in her.

And so we have faith, hope, and love, these three; but the greatest of these is love—the love of a Christian mother.

Chicken Salad

Mix together lightly: 2 cups diced *cooked chicken*, 1 cup finely chopped *celery*, ½ teaspoon *salt*, 1 teaspoon grated *onion*, 1 tablespoon *lemon juice*, ½ cup toasted *walnut pieces*, 3 *hard-boiled eggs*, diced, 1 cup *mayonnaise*, a handful of shredded *lettuce*. Chill and serve on lettuce leaves.

Jewel Platter

Cut a *honeydew melon* in half lengthwise, scoop out seeds. Dissolve 1 package *raspberry Jell-O* in 1 cup *boiling water*, stirring well. Stir in 1 package *frozen raspberries*. Chill until partially set. Fill hollows in melon with *Jell-O* mixture. Chill at least 4 hours. Slice each melon half in 3 slices, wiping blade between cuts. Place in spoke pattern on large serving platter and fill center of spoke and between slices with *green grape clusters*. Garnish with *lemon slices*.

Orange Rolls

Heat 1 cup *milk* to lukewarm. Put in bowl with 3 tablespoons *margarine*, ½ cup *sugar*, ½ teaspoon *salt,* and 1 package *dry yeast.* Let stand 3 minutes. Beat in 3 *eggs,* and 1 cup *flour.* Add 3½ cups more *flour* and beat well. Knead 10 minutes. Place in greased bowl, turning once to grease dough. Cover. Let rise 2 hours in warm place. Divide dough in half. Roll each half to 12" x 18" rectangle.

Combine 12 tablespoons *butter or margarine,* 1 cup *sugar,* and 1 tablespoon *grated orange peel.* Spread half over each rectangle of dough. Roll up, starting with long side. Slice each roll into 18 pieces. Place in two 9" x 9" pans and let rise 1½ hours. Bake at 375° for 15 minutes.

While they bake combine ¾ cup *sugar,* ½ cup *sour cream,* 3 tablespoons *orange juice,* and ½ cup *butter or margarine.* Boil, stirring constantly for 3 minutes. Pour over hot rolls.

Spring Flower Cake

First, make a French sponge cake layer, called Genoise and pronounced "jhenwahz." Place 3 *eggs* and ½ cup *sugar* in a large mixing bowl and set the bowl over a pan of hot water. Beat at high speed of electric mixer for about 15 minutes until triple in volume and a ribbon forms when beaters are lifted. Alternately fold in ½ cup *flour* and 2 tablespoons melted *butter.* Pour batter into a greased 8" cake pan. Bake at 375° for 10 minutes. Reduce heat to 350° and bake 10 minutes longer. Cool.

For frosting combine ½ cup *sugar,* 2 *egg whites,* and 2 tablespoons *water* in a double boiler. Beat with electric mixer over boiling water until soft peaks form. Add a 7-oz. jar *marshmallow cream* and beat to stiff peaks. Remove from heat and beat in ½ teaspoon *vanilla* and several drops *yellow food coloring.*

Split cake layer. Place bottom layer on large serving platter. Fill between layers and frost top and sides of cake with icing.

Make daisy decorations: Dip scissors in water and cut 5 *large marshmallows* vertically into 4 petals each. Arrange each 4 petals in a swirl, slightly overlapping, cut each petal in half again. Place a *small yellow gumdrop* in center.

For leaves, spray a sheet of waxed paper with *Pam* and roll several *small green gumdrops* between folds of paper with rolling pin. With fingers, pull each gum drop in half and curve a bit to resemble a leaf. Place around daisies.

Place 3 daisies on top of cake, one on the side, and another at the base.

Postscript

And if you think *you're* frantic, just read this "Receet For Washing Clothes" given to a new bride by her mother in 1908:

1. Bild fire in back yard to het kettle of rain water.
2. Set tubs so smoke won't blow in eyes if wind is peart.
3. Shave 1 hole cake lie sope in biling water.
4. Sort things. Make 3 piles. 1 pile white. 1 pile cullord. 1 pile work.
5. Stur flour in cold water to smooth then thin down with bilin water.
6. Rub dirty spots on board, scrub hard, then bile.

7. Rub cullord but don't bile, just rench and starch.
8. Take white things out of kettle with broom handle, then rench.
9. Spread tee towels on grass.
10. Hang old rags on fence.
11. Pore rench water on flower beds.
12. Scrub porch with hot sopy water.
13. Turn tubs upside down.
14. Go put on cleen dress—smooth hair with side combs, brew a cup of tea—set and rest and rock a spell and count blessings.

Oops, there's the buzzer. Time to put another load in the dryer.

INDEX